HOW LAWS ARE WRITTEN AND APPLIED

Bilika H. Simamba

LLB, LLM (Zambia), LLM in Legislation (Ottawa)
Advocate of the High Court for Zambia
Senior Legislative Counsel, Cayman Islands

authorHOUSE®

AuthorHouse™
1663 Liberty Drive
Bloomington, IN 47403
www.authorhouse.com
Phone: 1-800-839-8640

First published by AuthorHouse 3/31/2010

ISBN: 978-1-4490-7544-6 (e)
ISBN: 978-1-4490-7543-9 (sc)
ISBN: 978-1-4490-7545-3 (hc)

Library of Congress Control Number: 2010900494

Printed in the United States of America
Bloomington, Indiana

This book is printed on acid-free paper.

DEDICATION

For
My Parents
Gibson Chakwana Muchindu Simamba
and
Eddeth Makambe Kabwaya Simamba

CONTENTS

Cases Cited   xi

Legislation Cited   xv

Foreword   xxiii

Preface   xxv

Acknowledgements   xxix

Chapter 1 General Introduction   1

1.1 Criticisms of legislative language   1

1.2 How did legislation become so complex?   1

1.3 Can legislation be simplified?   3

1.4 The plain English movement   9

1.5 The purpose of this publication   12

Chapter 2 Drafting of Laws   15

2.1 Introduction   15

2.2 The legislative sentence: George Coode's analysis   17

2.3 Amendments   19

2.4 Avoiding ambiguity   30

2.4.1 Some basic drafting rules   30

2.4.1.1 Draft in the singular   30

2.4.1.2 Use the same word or expression for the same thing   31

2.4.1.3 Confer a power or impose a duty by
    active voice   32

2.4.2 Problematic words   32

2.4.2.1 "From" and "to"; "commencing" and "ending"   32

2.4.2.2 "Above" and "below"; "over" and "under"   33

2.4.2.3 "Less than" and "more than"; "not
    exceeding" and "exceeding"   33

2.4.2.4 "Despite", "notwithstanding" and "subject to"   35

2.4.2.5 "And" and "or"   38

2.4.2.6 "Shall", "may" and "must"   42

2.4.2.7 "In accordance with"   43

2.4.3 Contextual ambiguity   44

2.4.4 Ambiguity in general   45

2.4.4.1 Ambiguous modification   48

2.4.4.2 Date, age and time   58

2.4.4.3 Clauses starting with "because" and "without" 63

2.4.4.4 Other aspects of ambiguity: Cross-
    referencing   63

2.4.5 Other ways of promoting understanding   67

2.4.5.1 Double negatives   67

2.4.5.2 Indenting and chapeaux   68

2.4.5.3 Punctuation   71

2.5 General linguistic and other points   77

2.5.1 Verb tense   81

2.5.2 "The provisions of"   82

2.5.3 Statutory bodies   82

2.5.4 Crime provisions   87

2.5.5 Definition of terms   88

2.5.6 Gender-neutral laws   92

2.6 Structural check   94

Chapter 3 Interpretation of Statutes   105

3.1 Introduction   105

3.2 Supremacy of Parliament and of the constitution   107

3.2.1 General   107

3.2.2 Intention of Parliament   109

3.3 Rules of statutory interpretation   111

3.3.1 The mischief rule   111

3.3.2 The literal rule   112

3.3.3. The golden rule   112

3.3.4 The latest approach   113

3.4 Contradictions among rules of interpretation   118

3.4.1 Interpretation of statutory instruments   119

3.4.2 Some specific rules   122

3.4.2.1 In which cases do laws bind the state?   122

3.4.2.2 International law and national law   123

3.4.2.3 How new laws affect existing rights   129

3.4.2.4 Consistency of language   131

3.4.2.5 General words at the end of an enumeration (*ejusdem generis* rule)   132

3.4.2.6 Associated words (*noscitur a sociis*)   133

3.4.2.7 Technical words   134

3.4.2.8 Acts that are read narrowly   135

3.4.2.9 Tautology   136

3.4.2.10 Use of materials outside the law to understand the law   137

3.4.2.11 Errors and gaps   141

Chapter 4 Final Thought   149

Bibliography   151

Further Reading   153

Index   157

Cases Cited

Acting Commissioner of Police v. Bryan
(1985) WIR 207   3.4.2.2, n28

Adler v George [1964] 2 QB 7   3.4.2.11

Attorney General and 2 Ors v Joseph and Boyce CCJ
Appeal No. CV 2 of 2005; BB Civil Appeal No. 29 of 2004   3.4.2.2

Attorney General for Canada v. Attorney General for
Ontario (1937) AC 326   3.4.2.2

Baker v Canada (Minister of Citizenship and
Immigration) [1999] 2 SCR 817   3.4.2.2, n35

Black v Black 205 FLR 137   3.3.4

B v B [2008] FamCAFC 7   3.3.4, n14

Board of Inland Revenue v Young (Selwyn) (1997) 53
WIR 335   2.5.5

Bourne (Inspector of Taxes) v. Norwich Crematorium
[1967] 2 All ER 576   3.4.2.6

Caldow Properties Ltd v HJG Lowe and Associates Ltd
[1971] NZLR 131   2.5.5, n34

Cape Brandy Syndicate v Inland Revenue
Commissioners [1921] 1 KB 64, CA   3.4.2.8, n41

Canada Ltée (Spraytech Société d'arrosage v
Hudson(Town)[2001] 2 SCR 241   3.4.2.2, n35

Chief Adjudication Officer v. Foster [1993] AC 754   3.4.2.10

C.O. Williams Construction Ltd v Blackman and
Another (1994) 45 WIR 94   2.4.1.1, n12

de Freitas v Permanent Secretary for the Ministry of
Agriculture, Fisheries, Lands and Housing and Others
[1998] 53 WIR 133   3.3.4, n20

Douglas (Clayton) v The Police (1992) 43 WIR 175   2.4.5.3, n32

DPP v. Schildcamp (1971) AC 1   3.2.2

Ealing London Borough Council v. Race Relations
Board [1972] AC 342   3.3.4

Ebanks (A.G.) v R (2007) CILR 403, Ct of Appeal,
Cayman   3.4.2.3, n36

Fraser v Greenaway (1992) 41 WIR 136   3.3.4, n20

Garland v British Rail Engineering Limited [1983] 2
AC 751   3.4.2.2, n35

Grey v. Pearson (1857) 6 HLC 61   3.3.3

Heydon's Case (1584) 3 Co Rep 7a; 76 ER 637   3.3.1

Hill v. William Hill (Park Lane Ltd) (1949) AC 530   3.4.2.9

Hydes (R) v Attorney-General (2000) CILR 206,
Grand Ct, Cayman   3.3.3, n11

Magor and St. Mellons Rural District Council v.
Newport Corp. [1950] 2 All E R 1226, at 1236, CA   3.3.4, n21

Mills v Meeking (1990) 169 CLR 214   3.3.4

Murray v. Director of Public Prosecutions [1994] 1 WLR 1 — 3.4.2.10, n44

Pepper v. Hart [1992] 3 WLR 1032 — 3.3.4, .4.2.10

Pfizer Canada v Canada (Attorney General) (2003) 224 DLR (4th) 178 — 3.4.2.2, n35

Pratt and Morgan v Attorney General of Jamaica (1993) 43 WIR 340; [1994] 2 AC 1 — 3.4.2.2

Prestcold Central Ltd v. Minister of Labour [1969] 1 WLR 89 — 3.4.2.9, n43

Reference Re Public Service Employer Relations Act (Alberta) [1987] 1 SCR 313 — 3.4.2.2, 35

Regina v Secretary of State for Home Department, ex parte Brind and Ors [1991] AC 696 — 3.4.2.2, n 35

Rao v. Attorney General, Supreme Court of Zambia Appeal No 24 of 1987 — 3.4.2.6

Richardson and Others v Richardson (1995) 50 WIR 178 — 3.4.2.3, 36

Royal College of Nursing v. Department of Health (1981) 1 All E R 545 — 3.2.2

R v Shubley [1990] SCR 3 — 3.4.2.11

Rumbolt v. Schmidt (1882) 8 QBD 603 — 3.4.2.8, n40

Seaford Court Estates v Asher [1949] 2 KB 481 — 1.3, n6

Stockdale v. Hansard (1839) 9 Ad and E 1; 112 ER 1112; 48 Rev Rep 326 — 3.4.2.10, n44

Stubbings v. Webb [1993] AC 498 . 3.4.2.10

Sussex Peerage Case (1844) 11 CL & Fin 85; 8 ER
1034 3.3.2

Tavita v Minister of Immigration [1994] 2 NZLR 257 3.4.2.2, n35

The Beta (1869) 3 Moo. PC (NS) 23 3.2.1.11

Van Gend en Loos v. Nederlandse Administratie der
Belastingen (1963) ECR 1 3.4.2.2

Yew Bon Tew v Kenderaan Bas Mera [1982] 3 All ER
833 3.4.2.3

Legislation Cited

Australia [Aust]

Acts Interpretation Act 1901

s 14A	2.3
s 15AB (1)	3.4.2.10
s 15AB (2)	3.4.2.10
s 15AB (3)	3.4.2.10
s 18B (1)	2.5.6
s 18B (2)	2.5.6
s 23 (a)	2.5.6
s 23 (b)	2.4.1.1, n11
s 35	2.4.4.2, n27
s 36	2.4.4.2, n27
s 37	2.4.4.2, n27
s 46 (1)	3.4.1, n23
s 46 (2)	3.4.1, n23

Family Law Act 1975

s 90 (G) (1) (b)	3.4.4

Acts Interpretation Amendment Act 1980

s 15AA	3.3.4

Australian Capital Territory [ACT]

Human Rights Amendment Act 2008   2.3

Barbados [Bbdos]

Barbados Independence Order 1966 No 1455

s 1   3.2.1, n1

s 78   3.4.2.2

British Virgin Islands [BVI]

Criminal Code 1997

s 20   2.4.1.1

Income Tax Act Cap 206

s 25   2.4.2.3, n13

Income Tax (Amendment) Act No 11 of 1996

s 2   2.4.2.3, n13

Virgin Islands (Constitution) (Amendment) Order 2000
UKSI No 1343

s 2 (1)   2.3

s 2 (2)   2.3

Virgin Islands (Constitution) Order 1976 UKSI No
2145   2.3

Virgin Islands (Constitution) Order 2007 UKSI No
1678   2.3

Canada [Can]

Interpretation Act Chapter 1-21

s 2 (1)	3.4.1
s 11	2.4.2.6
s 16	3.4.1
s 17	3.4.2.1, n24
s 21 (1)	2.5.3
s 21 (2)	2.5.3
s 21 (3)	2.5.3
s 26 (1)	2.4.4.2
s 27 (1)	2.4.4.2
s 27 (2)	2.4.4.2
s 27 (3)	2.4.4.2
s 27 (4)	2.4.4.2
s 27 (5)	2.4.4.2
s 28	2.4.4.2
s 29	2.4.4.2
s 30	2.4.4.2

s 33 (1)   2.5.6

s 33 (2)   2.4.1.1

s 40 (2)   2.3, n7

Correctional Services Act   3.4.2.11

Dominica [Dom]

Commonwealth of Dominica Constitution Order 1978
UKSI No 1027

s 117   3.2.1, n1

Jamaica [Jam]

Jamaica (Constitution) Order in Council 1962 UKSI No
1550

s 15   3.4.2.2

New Zealand [NZ]

Interpretation Act 1999

s 6   2.5.1, n33

s 8 (2)   2.4.4.2, n25

s 9 (2)   2.4.4.2, n25

s 23   2.3, n7

s 27	3.4.2.1, n25
s 29	2.3, n7
s 31	2.5.6
s 34	3.4.1

Ontario [Ont]

Bees Act

s 25	2.4.2.5, n17

Charitable Institutions Act

s 12 (1)	2.4.2.5, n18

Trinidad and Tobago [TT]

Constitution of Trinidad and Tobago Act No 4 of 1976

s 2	3.2.1, n1

United Kingdom [UK]

European Communities Act 1972

s 2 (1)	3.4.2.2
s 2 (2)	3.4.2.2
s 3 (1)	3.4.2.2

Interpretation Act 1978

s 6 (a)   2.5.6, n40

s 6 (b)   2.5.6, n40

s11   3.4.1

Merchant Shipping Act 1854

s 374   3.4.2.11

Trade Union and Labour Relations Act 1992

s 229 (4)   2.4.5 (b)

United States of America [USA]

Constitution of the United States of America

Art VI   3.2.1, n1

Zambia [Zam]

Constitution of Zambia

s 80 (1)   3.2.1

Interpretation Act Cap 2

s 4 (2)   2.5.6, n40

s 4 (3)   2.4.1.1, n11

s 12   2.3

s 16   2.3

s 20 (2)   3.4.1, n22

s 35   2.4.4.2

s 51 (1)   3.4.2.1

FOREWORD

Lawyers are said to be master wordsmiths. Whereas generally speaking this cannot be doubted, lawyers also face much criticism for the verbiage and legalese that has been traditional in the legal profession. The criticism is that unnecessary or far-fetched words often cloud the communication of otherwise simple ideas; even where the concept is more complex and difficult, the ordinary lay reader might not be expected to be anymore sympathetic to or accommodating of abstruse language. However, generally speaking laws are well-drafted but problems of clear and succinct drafting remain.

In recent years there has been a proliferation of books and articles advocating the use of plain language in legal documents, including written laws. These materials are aimed not only at making the case for writing in plain English but also providing the skills necessary to achieve it. The push for changes in approaches to the drafting of legal documents has been a central aim of the so-called "plain English movement". These efforts have helped to reduce the sometimes undue complexity of language used in such writing. The author, who is an experienced legislative drafter, validates much of the criticism of legislative language while explaining that some of it is misplaced. In this book he seeks to give practical application to the call for simplification of legislative drafting.

The ability to communicate efficiently in writing is a skill that everybody needs. An official in government or outside cannot write a clear memorandum, report or other document unless they have excellent writing skills. In writing legislation or, indeed, even for understanding legislation, one needs not just writing and comprehension skills but also a good knowledge of certain legal rules that have been developed by the courts on how to read and understand a statute. These rules are ever changing and can make for very complex and sometimes conflicting application. The author also offers explanations for how the main rules have evolved and where they are today. In explaining them he does well to refer to a sampling of cases from the United Kingdom, Canada, Australia, New Zealand and the Caribbean.

I have no doubt that this book will benefit law students, budding attorneys, civil servants and members of the public who wish to fine tune their writing skills and better understand the import of any statute that affects them or which they may be implementing. Even the experienced lawyer will find cases and insightful opinions that are relevant to his practice.

The Hon. Anthony Smellie Q.C.; J.P;
LL.D (Hon.) Liverpool; LL.B (Hons) (U.W.I.); CLE.
Chief Justice, Grand Court, Cayman Islands

5th October, 2009

PREFACE

In order for a public official to craft an optimum partnership with the lawyer who drafts laws, he needs three things. First, he has to know the legislative process and how to play his role in it. Second, it is necessary for him to be equipped with some knowledge of how laws are drafted and why they are drafted in a certain way. Unless he has at least some basic knowledge of approaches to drafting, his ability to comment meaningfully on legislation will be limited. Third and related to the second, the official needs an understanding of the rules of statutory interpretation, which are taken into account in drafting legislation.

In the book *The Legislative Process: A Handbook for Public Officials* (Bloomington, Indiana: AuthorHouse, 2009) I dealt with the first of these. However, in the larger scheme of things, especially in developing jurisdictions, that is not enough. It is not enough because there the instructing official has to shape proposals and make comments on draft legislation often without the help of a departmental solicitor. My philosophy is that for a government to expand legislative drafting capacity to the maximum level, it is necessary for the official in such a jurisdiction to be armed with enough knowledge to enable him to operate virtually as a legislative assistant to Legislative Counsel. In other words, in order to be an instructing officer-cum-legislative assistant, he has to understand not only the legislative process but also have basic word-handling skills that the drafting of legislation needs. He also needs to understand some basics of how legislation is interpreted. I hope that this, the Simamba Philosophy on the Drafting and Other Handling of Legislation, will help to change perspectives of what is possible, even in the context of the critical shortage of drafters in developing jurisdictions.

Unfortunately, there are few materials written in such a way as to make legislative drafting and the interpretation of statutes palatable not only to law students and lawyers but also to non-lawyers. Whereas there are many standard published works on legislative drafting and the interpretation of statutes which contain a lot of information that would be useful to a layperson, they have their limitations. The bulk of books on legislative drafting are meant for lawyers who draft laws or are training to draft, while books on statutory interpretation are generally meant for students of law or lawyers. Also, usually one book is dedicated to each of the two areas. As a result, books on these subjects often have a lot of information that is not frequently needed by the public official or which, even if needed, is presented with too much detail or jargon, at least from the lay official's vantage point. Consequently, they are unattractive to him, as he has to rummage through a mass of information before he finds what he actually needs. This publication is intended to meet that need in a more efficient way in that it deals with both drafting and interpretation in a less voluminous rendition.

When an official has a reasonable knowledge of drafting and interpretation, he can better tell whether a provision has the effect that he has requested the drafter to give it and whether that effect is readily discernible. That way he can better assist the drafter in perfecting drafts. In order to do this, the instructing official needs, in some measure, to delve into some of the rules and competencies in which a drafter is involved daily. The official will also find that it is important to have working knowledge of certain simple but useful and frequently applied rules on the interpretation of legislation, some of which will be found in an Interpretation Act and others in leading court cases. Without a cadre of officials who have a reasonable knowledge of approaches to the drafting and interpretation of laws, it is difficult to deliver legislation that is conceptually sound and of high editorial quality. In most developing jurisdictions, emphasis has been placed on training drafters but not on helping officials to understand how legislation is drafted and impart skills to them that allow officials to comment on legislation meaningfully.

In relation specifically to statutory interpretation, the general position in the British Commonwealth is that each statute will state how it is to be interpreted. For example, a statute may define what is meant by "house" in that particular Act. If it does not, one has to consult the Interpretation Act to see if there is a definition of that term. If that Act does not define the term, the court will assign meaning in the light of the context in which it is used, a process in which previously decided cases may play a part. It is, therefore, important for the official to familiarize himself with the Interpretation Act in his jurisdiction. It will often decipher apparently complex or unclear statutory provisions. Where one cannot readily find their own Interpretation Act, I recommend a reading of the Interpretation Act 1999 of New Zealand, which was updated in 2008. It can be accessed by Google or other search engine. This will give the reader an idea of what to expect in his own Act. I chose it not only because it typifies an Interpretation Act but also because it is a great example of how clarity can be achieved with few words.

The gamut of officials who are expected to benefit from this book include:

(a) persons who are undertaking courses in legal drafting;

(b) law students at certificate or degree level who wish to have nutshell exposure to some basics of how laws are written and applied, or are taking a course in legal writing or the interpretation of statutes;

(c) lawyers learning how to draft laws either on the job or in residential or long-distance institutions, and drafters who wish to expand their knowledge of drafting or the interpretation of statutes;

(d) law officers and other officials in international organizations who work with governments to help such governments enact legislation arising out of international obligations;

(e) Cabinet ministers and legislators, who need the ability to read and understand draft or enacted legislation;

(f) public officials such as permanent secretaries, deputy permanent secretaries, assistant secretaries, heads of department and other senior officials, who review or apply legislation;

(g) senior persons in quasi-government organizations, especially statutory corporations, who may request amendments to their governing statutes or their complete review and who thereafter have to review the draft legislation or apply it once enacted;

(h) law officers in government who advise on the application of legislation and may participate in making legislative proposals and therefore reviewing of draft laws;

(i) officials outside government such as those in non-governmental organizations (NGOs) who review draft legislation that they have requested;

(j) lawyers outside government who often have opportunities to undertake consultancies drafting laws but lack the necessary skills to write clear legislation.

The book comprises principally three chapters. Chapter 1 addresses the issue of complexity of laws and what is being done about it in different parts of the world. Chapter 2 deals with legislative drafting while chapter 3 discusses the rules of statutory interpretation. The latter contains the concepts which I found came up most frequently when dealing with officials who were working with me to produce legislation.

BHS
George Town
Grand Cayman
Cayman Islands
British West Indies
September, 2009
bsimamba@yahoo.co.uk

ACKNOWLEDGEMENTS

First, I would like to thank Mr. Justice Anthony Smellie, QC, Chief Justice of the Cayman Islands, for agreeing to write the foreword for this publication. I also thank Attorney General Sam Bulgin, QC, and Solicitor General Cheryll Richards for their support. I am grateful to Claudette Upton for her comments on parts of chapter 2. Peter Barrett, formerly Senior Legislative Drafting Officer with the New South Wales Parliamentary Counsel's Office, was most welcoming of my importunate demands to share with me some of his views and information on practices. For that I am grateful to him. I also thank my colleagues in the Legislative Drafting Department and the Law Reform Commission for a fruitful exchange of ideas.

In the writing of this book I benefited greatly from a number of leading works in the field. Among these I should mention specifically those of G. C. Thornton, Robert C. Dick, Elmer A. Driedger and F. Reed Dickerson. They are cited elsewhere in this book.

My gratitude also goes out to Mwangala Simamba for her assistance in proofreading part of the manuscript. However, if any imperfections remain, they are all entirely mine.

Chapter 1
General Introduction

1.1 Criticisms of legislative language

If you think that legislative language is too difficult to understand, you are in good company. Some of its sharpest critics are judges. A judge once said, in effect, about a statute that was before him, that if the intention of the drafter was to absolutely confuse and bamboozle anyone who read it, that aim had been achieved. Extreme criticisms, however, are rare and I will address the issue further in this chapter.

Generally speaking, many criticisms of legislative language (and legal language in general) are valid. Whereas popular language in general continues to evolve, legislative language seems always to lag behind. Words and expressions that have long been abandoned in ordinary speech and even in some formal writing live on in legislative circles and in written laws. As a result, some of that language becomes known as legal language when it is nothing but old or convoluted English.

1.2 How did legislation become so complex?

In England legislation was not always drafted in English. It was drafted in Latin for a while then in Norman French. Thereafter the era of drafting laws in English followed. This shift contributed to the verbosity of legislative language. When laws were drafted in Norman French, precedents of laws drafted in Latin were used. During those years a drafter often had to decide whether a word or concept in Latin had an exact equivalent in Norman French. If he was not sure, out of abundance of caution, he used two or three words in Norman French. Similar considerations applied when the transition to English drafting occurred. A drafter had to decide if a word in English sufficiently captured a concept used in Latin, Norman French or both. However, history is only part of the problem: The fact that lawyers were paid by the number of words they used played more than just a small part in this approach.

Today we do not have to deal with legal concepts in Norman French. We have to deal with some Latin but nowhere near the amount of Norman French that lawyers in those days had to deal with. Indeed, Latin is being phased out as lawyers, legislative drafters in particular, prefer to use English terms where there is an exact equivalent. Regarding verbosity, even today it is not entirely unknown that a lawyer will produce a voluminous document for reasons related more to the size of the bill than to the needs of the client.

And yet all these reasons are a very small part of the reason why laws are complex. Where a particular provision has been used for decades or even centuries and has been found to work, lawyers will continue to use it even if the language later appears dated. This is more so where there are court cases that have held the provision to have a particular meaning. Such provisions acquire a kind of respectable antiquity and lawyers therefore feel that they can change them only at their own peril. Even if they were inclined to modernize a provision, the time it would take to research the full legal effect of that provision and ensure that any change does not result in substantive deviation from the meaning of the precedent is often considered to be unnecessary. Even that is not the whole story.

1.3 CAN LEGISLATION BE SIMPLIFIED?

Few people outside the legislative drafting profession understand what is involved in the drafting of laws. People will be heard to say that drafters put legislative proposals into "legal language". A draft is sometimes put before the drafter so that he can put it on "firmer legal footing" or the drafter who is presented with a draft is asked to raise only "drafting points". Such statements reveal an insufficient appreciation of what drafting involves and the factors that affect complexity of legislation. What is more, the term "drafter" does not help for it underplays the legal advice role and other challenges that come with the function of Legislative Counsel.

The first thing to understand about the complexity or otherwise of legislation is that drafting of a law is inextricably bound with the concepts involved. Before putting pen to paper, the sponsors of legislation have to conceptualize their proposals in detail. Then the drafter has to try and gain a deep understanding of the proposals. Almost invariably in this process, he will need clarifications on various points. And as a result of his inquiries, even good proposals may require refinement. Sometimes he may identify flaws that require comprehensive review of the proposals or, in some cases, abandonment of the proposed legislation. For a drafter who already has the requisite drafting skills, conceptualizing can be a more difficult task than actual drafting.

Not all laws can be simplified to a level where every reasonably educated person, let alone every person, can understand them. A matter can only be simplified to the extent allowable by its subject matter. Thus it has been said that: "Some statutes are, indeed, frightfully complicated, but it is not the draftsman who made them so. Laws must sometimes be enacted to deal with very complex situations and obviously no one can understand the Statute unless he understands those situations."[1] Certain subjects relating to wills, land, companies, contracts, taxes, accounting

3

and scores of other issues cannot be reduced to a kind of Janet-and-John simplicity.

Then there is the confusion between drafting flaws and policy deficiencies. One commentator has said:

> There is a tendency to regard Parliamentary Counsel as the root of all legislative evil, or at least as the source of all legislative obscurity and prolixity. In debates in Parliament one will frequently hear the drafting nominally attacked where the speaker is actually taking exception to the substance of the provision concerned.[2]

A law may contain a provision that states that "A person facing a possible assault has an obligation to take to his heels." This may be a very bad law but is reasonably plain in drafting terms.

Also, a general criticism of drafting ability is sometimes made on the basis of an isolated and exotic case. Because many laws are quite clear, they are applied in thousands and even millions of cases without difficulty. It is usually when a rare case arises that the competence of the drafter is called into question. Unfortunately, his competence is then called into question in sometimes wholesale fashion.

The saving grace is that there is understanding from informed high places. The Renton Committee put things in the right perspective when it said:

> Even in the face of such difficulties many statutes are well drafted and give no grounds for criticism in respect of clarity and simplicity; indeed some of our witnesses have praised the drafting of a number of recent Acts. Not all of the criticism we have heard in relation to particular Acts has turned out, on close examination, to be entirely valid. Nevertheless, after making due allowance, there remains cause for concern that difficulty is be-

ing encountered by the ultimate users of statutes, and this difficulty increases as the statute book continues to grow.[3]

In addition, legislation is often drafted under very tight time constraints. Though many governments do have well developed procedures
to ensure, as much as possible, that drafters have enough time to do
their work properly, it is not always possible to have the ideal amount of
time needed to draft legislation. And even where legislative procedures
that are conducive to an efficient system exist, insufficient knowledge of
those procedures or a lack of appreciation of how much time is needed
to craft a good piece of legislation still pose challenges for the drafter.
These problems are often exacerbated by major changes that are introduced late in the drafting process or during consideration by legislative
bodies. Whether the changes are major in terms of a new key concept or
a number of unrelated changes, all late changes come with a greater risk
of conceptual and clerical errors.

In some cases an attempt by a drafter to make a matter clear is often
met with opposition from instructing officials or legislators who for one
reason or another think it unnecessary or would like to leave it deliber-
ately vague for their own operational convenience. Then there are those
who just feel more comfortable with conservative language and verbosity
and those who fear that simpler expression will water down their liveli-
hood.

Whatever detractors might say, the following continues to be true:

There is little doubt that most of the new features that are in-
tensely disliked by linguistic conservatives will triumph in the
end. But the language will not bleed to death. Nor will it seem
in any way distorted once the old observances have been forgotten.[4]

There is no shortage of prescriptions as to what we should try to achieve. The following is particularly poignant:

> If a man were to ask me what I would suppose to be a perfect style of language, I would answer, that in which a man speaking to five hundred people, of all common and various capacities, idiots or lunatics expected, should be understood by them all, and in the same sense which the speaker intended to be understood.[5]

This is certainly an ideal and yet Utopian aim. Whereas there are certain particularly simple subject matters where this can be attempted and achieved to a large degree, most legislation cannot be simplified to that level. What the drafter attempts to do is craft provisions in such a way as to make them readily understandable to the audience to which the law is addressed.

Even if one where to draft a statute that is addressed to the ordinary person and express it in language that comes close to the Utopian aim cited above, there is no guarantee that it will always be easy to apply to all circumstances. Thus it has been rightly said that:

> Whenever a statute comes up for consideration it must be remembered that it is not within human powers to foresee the manifold sets of facts which may arise, and, even if it were, it is not possible to provide for them in terms free from all ambiguity. The English language is not an instrument of mathematical precision. Our literature would be much the poorer if it were. This is where the draftsmen of Acts of Parliament have often been unfairly criticized.[6]

In this regard, a drafter's role is often to draft a general rule that will apply to certain classes of situation. In so doing, the rule may be absolute or be subject to exceptions. In formulating a rule, there is either one particular kind of case being addressed or a class of cases. Some rules are relatively simple. For example, rules of procedure may provide that where a chairman is unable to attend, the vice-chairman shall chair the meeting. However, many rules are aimed at addressing situations that cannot all be individually stated.

Therefore:

> A provision that is difficult to understand must be seen not as an inability on the part of the drafter to express himself in terms free from ambiguity, but rather as a display of his ability to foresee the many possible situations that may arise and his attempt to express himself as clearly as possible in relation to those situations, using tools that lack mathematical precision. Any other conclusion is likely to involve the absurdity that a lawyer loses much of his ability to express himself clearly when he engages in the preparation of legislation.[7]

Thus even if a drafter were to observe all the factors that contribute to the ready conveyance of his meaning, the situations at the back of his mind which he wants to cater for may make for a complicated provision.

For now we can agree that legislation is supposed to be communication. To that extent it is no different from the spoken word. In that connection it has been said that:

> The final cause of speech is to get an idea as exactly as possible out of one mind into another. Its formal cause therefore is such choice and disposition of words as will achieve this end most economically.[8]

The aim of legislation should be the same.

Quite apart from the challenges stated above, the drafter sometimes has to deal with his own habits. Even if he is dealing with clients who are amenable to change and he too is equally amenable to it, the literary legal tradition to which he was exposed as a student and later as a practitioner imbued in him certain literary habits. As a student he crammed certain words and styles day and night. If he did not specifically try to learn them, they grew on him, for much of what he read was written that way.

When trying to give a precedent a more modern rendering, he has to re-think the meaning of certain words and concepts, and then find a more current way of saying the same thing. That is why drafting legislation in plain English takes longer than to draft it in old language. Extricating oneself from an archaic way of writing is a major and on-going process.

If, therefore, a drafter is willing to write legislation that is plain, how is he to be guided? In the first place one has to use their common sense as to what would make a piece of writing easy to understand. Some of the more obvious things that improve understanding are good organization of the material, simple sentence structure and careful word choice. Today there are numerous materials published by governments and the private sector that assist or claim to assist in attempts to write in plain English.[9]

Whereas ordinary people and even scholars have criticized the obscurity of lawyers' language for centuries, it was only in the 1970s that significant global effort was made to simplify the language of law. Until this time little or no effort was made in a concerted way to make language plain. The extent to which the language of law was remote from everyday usage is exemplified by the following short conversation in a court of law:

Judge: The charge is theft of frozen chickens. Are you the defendant?

Defendant: No, sir, I'm the guy who stole the chickens.[10]

Then you had the traditional writ of summons which required that the person being sued "enter an appearance" at a certain court house. People where known to show up at that address. They did not need to do this as such. Simply put, they were required to file, in person or through a lawyer, a document called an appearance or a memorandum of appearance in which they were required to indicate if they intended to defend the action in whole or in part. Happily, modern court documents now spell this out in less esoteric fashion.

Few legislative drafters today will argue with the proposition that we need to draft our laws in plain English. What then is plain English? The Law Reform Commission of Victoria, Australia, has said that:

> Plain English involves the use of plain, straightforward language which avoids defects and conveys its meaning as clearly and as simply as possible, without unnecessary pretension or embellishment. It is to be contrasted with convoluted, repetitive and prolix language. The adoption of a plain English style demands simply that a document be written in a style which readily conveys its message to its audience.[11]

1.4 THE PLAIN ENGLISH MOVEMENT

Governments and the private sector worldwide have been responding in varying degrees to calls to use plain English. Further to what has been mentioned above, in the United States the need to use plain language in legal documents or statutes can be found in the laws of New York, Connecticut, Pennsylvania, Florida, Minnesota and California.[12]

In Australia the government endorsed the plain English movement by introducing the Plain English and Simpler Forms Programme. This was followed by a number of departments introducing plain English initiatives. On the teaching side, in 1991 the Centre for Plain Legal Language was established at the University of Sidney. It researches and promotes the use of plain English in legal and administrative documents. An Australian who should know said in a speech delivered in 2002:

> Australian lawyers have been so enthusiastic about plain language that it is almost possible to argue . . . that the battle for acceptance of plain language is already won there. Certainly now, as a consultant, I am rarely asked to come to persuade law firms that plain language is safe (10 years ago I had to do regularly). Now the demand is for in-house training in plain language writing. And, interestingly, there is very little demand from law firms for consultants to come in and actually *rewrite* documents. The skills are already in the law firms. That seems like a healthy development . . . But it is also a sign that Australian lawyers feel *confident* that they know what they are doing and *believe* they can write in plain language. Plain language drafting *has* been taught in Australian law schools now for a decade.[13]

In 1971 the Law Reform Commission of Canada, which supports use of plain language, started examining federal laws with a view to recommending ways of making them easier to understand. Then in 1991 the Government of Canada published a manual on plain writing. This was based on the work of federal government departments. And in the bastion of formal and some will say convoluted English, the United Kingdom of Great Britain and Northern Ireland, a plain English policy was adopted in 1982. The government runs courses to assist public officials with designing and presenting complex information in a direct and simple manner.

Down Under, the New South Wales Parliamentary Counsel's Office embraced the principles of plain language from the early 1980s and formally adopted plain language as a policy in 1986 for all legislation. The office's adopted definition is that: "Plain Language is clear intelligible English. It is not simplistic English. It does not involve loss of precision."[14]

Plain language in the legislative context aims for "clarity in the language of legislation, in the structure of the legal ideas contained in legislation, and in the physical layout and presentation of legislation."[15] Indeed, this is the general understanding of plain language. In the words of one authority:

> When we draft in plain language we look at more than just the meaning of words we are using and how they will be perceived by our readers. We also look at how the information is organized and presented. We look at the *organization* of the words in a sentence, the sentences in a document and the *design and layout* of the document itself.[16]

It should suffice to say that the plain English movement has succeeded in fostering changes to legal language in ways never envisaged before though this success has not been universal or moved at the same pace in different parts of the world. In the midst of much progress, there are people still holding out. One still finds statement such as:

> Do not look for savings by trying to make the law easier for lay persons to understand. Instead, make it easier for lawyers to use. Plain English and reducing jargon have only a small part to play in this.[17]

This passage must have had a distinctly dated air even in 1995 when it was written. Law is intended to regulate the conduct of either the general populace or particular categories of the public. If everyone always or most of the time had to go to lawyers to comply with the law, society would be unworkable. The reduction of jargon will not make complex laws simple in terms of their concepts but it will allow reasonably intelligent people in the community to understand many laws without having to seek legal advice. Prolixity and obscurity of legal language have to be avoided because they often lead to undue inconvenience to the general public. What is more, many people who fail to understand a provision may not seek legal advice even if they can get it. They may simply adopt what they consider to be the more likely meaning of the provision with which they are dealing.

When legislation or any legal document is drafted in plain English, it is to the advantage of all in the long run. A lawyer who drafts a simple lease that his client can understand is likely to attract more clients. A bank whose agreements are in plain English is likely to be very competitive in the market. When a government drafts legislation in plain English, its officials are less likely to make mistakes in applying the legislation. Readily discernible meaning of such writing also saves the people concerned the frustration of having to seek legal advice frequently.

1.5 THE PURPOSE OF THIS PUBLICATION

This book deals with the word-handling skills necessary to write legislation effectively. In so doing, it embodies principles of plain language drafting. These word-handling skills are often taught as part of a course on the drafting of laws or legal drafting in general. However, as I have said above, the skills are essential not only to drafters of laws but also to any person who will ever write or read anything. They will help him to successfully convey or discern meaning, as the case may be. Further, the skills have to be coupled with certain rules governing the interpretation of statutes, some of which originate in rules of ordinary language.

The book is not principally concerned with the physical design of legislation. There are other publications that deal with this matter in detail.[18] For present purposes it should suffice to reiterate that in addition to clarity in actual drafting, communication of the contents of legislation is aided by the layout of legislation. Plain English cannot be achieved unless matters of layout are also sufficiently addressed.

Notes

1. Elmer A. Driedgar, *The Composition of Legislation* (Ottawa, Ontario: Department of Justice, 1976), pxxiii.

2. D. Greenberg, *Craies on Legislation: A Practitioners' Guide to the Nature, Process, Effect and Interpretation of Legislation*, 8th ed. (London: Sweet and Maxwell, 2004), 206.

3. Renton Committee, Cmmd. 6053 paras 61, 62. Quoted from V. R. A. C. Crabbe, *Legislative Drafting* (London: Cavendish, 1993), 54, 55.

4. Robert Burchfield. Quoted from Sir Ernest Gowers, *The Complete Plain Words*, 3rd ed. (London: H.M. Stationery Office, 1986; Harmondsworth: Penguin Books, 1987), 24. Citations are to the Penguin edition.

5. Defoe. Quoted from Gowers, n4, 10.

6. Denning L. J. *Seaford Court Estates Ltd v Asher* [1949] 2 K B 481, 498.

7. B. Simamba, "The Experiences of a Drafter in the Legislative Development of Zambia", Namibia Papers, Working Document No. 5, Part I, Centre for African Studies, University of Bremen, 51.

8. G. M. Young. Quoted from Gowers, n4, 1.

9. See for example *Legislation Manual: Structure and Style*. Report 35 (Wellington, N.Z.: Law Reform Commission, May 1996). Further, see the bibliography and further reading sections at the end of this book.

10. Found at http://www.languageandlaw.org/PLAINENGLISH.HTM. Quoted from Peter Tiersma, *The Plain English Movement*, where it is acknowledged to Robert Patterson, esq., of Santa Barbara 1. Accessed 10th November, 2007. Capitalization and italics removed.

11. *Plain English and the Law*. Report No. 9. (Melbourne, Victoria: Law Reform Commission of Victoria, 1987).

12. See contents at http://www.languageandlaw.org/TEXTS/STATS/ PLAINENG.HTM.

13. Asprey, Recent Developments in the Plain Language Movement in Australia, a paper presented to the Fourth Biennial Conference of the PLAIN Language Association International, September 27, 2002, Toronto, Canada, 1, 2.

14. Accessed from http://www.pco.nsw.gov.au/about.htm on 13 March, 2008. See link "plain language" to find *New South Wales Parliamentary Counsel's Office, Policies relating to Plain Language and gender-neutral expression*, May 2000, 1.

15. Ibid.

16. Michèle Asprey, *Plain Language for Lawyers*, 3rd ed. (Sydney: Federation Press, 2003), 13. See also at p 11 where she says "Some people think that plain language is simple, it must be simplistic – a kind of baby-talk. That is also wrong. Simple in this sense doesn't mean simplistic. It means straightforward, clear, precise."

17. Quoted from www.francisbennion.com as at 10 November, 2007. Originally from Francis Bennion, *Don't Put the Law into Public Hands*, The Times, January 24th 1995.

18. Refer to Asprey, n16, Chap 15 "Document design basics" and Chap 16 "Designing documents for the computer screen".

Chapter 2
Drafting of Laws

2.1 Introduction

Parliamentary Counsel generally prefer not to receive from the instructing official a draft of the proposed legislation but rather a narrative statement of the proposals being made. The problem is that, being the rare species they are, Parliamentary Counsel, especially in developing jurisdictions, have to work in particularly understaffed departments. As a result, they normally do not have lots of time. One solution that has been proposed is training laypersons in the drafting of laws, and attempts have even been made to offer such training. It must be admitted that in some cases a non-drafter can prepare a simple draft on a simple matter that, if it is largely properly done and fully explained, may save Parliamentary Counsel some time and enable him to finalize the matter sooner than would have been the case otherwise. Whereas this book does not aim to make a layperson a drafter, it can go a long way to help him develop a degree of legislative penmanship. For a non-drafter to have a realistic chance of producing a useful draft, and to be able to meaningfully review any drafts prepared by the drafter, in addition to discussing any proposed draft with the drafter before drafting begins,

15

the non-drafter needs some word-handling skills that are an essential part of the drafting of legislation.

It must be said that generally in the Commonwealth countries of Africa and Asia, English is not the first language; it is only the official language. Many professionals, therefore, had never spoken English when they first went to school or at least did not speak it frequently or very competently (although things are beginning to change). Usually, they spoke a native language. At school, however, English quickly became the medium of instruction, and gradually it came into frequent use in the office and even in social interaction. So-called standard English is not the norm either in the Commonwealth Caribbean, South Pacific countries and elsewhere. There also, it is only the official language. Even if in some of these countries the people are said to speak English, the fact is that they speak an informal English, which, from the vantage point of countries such as England, Australia and New Zealand, is considered "broken" or patois. The average child entering school speaks fluent informal English, and has to learn the rules of grammar from scratch and attempt to infuse them into everyday speech and writing. I hasten to add that many professionals in these countries eventually acquire a command of the language in their professions that is equal to that of professionals in the older Commonwealth. In summary, therefore, while it can be said that all Commonwealth countries are English-speaking, they are English-speaking in at least three different ways.

All that means that the civil servant in the newer Commonwealth has even greater challenges than his counterpart in the older cousin countries. My experience is that many public-service workers in the newer Commonwealth retain language deficiencies that affect their ability to understand legislation, let alone to prepare even a good layman's draft. Some deficiencies are not unknown even in the older Commonwealth.[1] It is hoped that this chapter will assist the official not just in preparing simple drafts and reviewing drafts meaningfully but also with writing skills in general. In writing this chapter, therefore, and indeed in writing the whole work, I have attempted to be as simple as possible, as the work is intended for a wide spectrum of public-service workers. Almost all the basic skills dealt with are relevant to writing not just legislation but also other documents in official circles. I hope that by presenting these skills in the context of a subject in which officials are directly interested – that is, legislation – I am making it more likely that the following exposition will be read.[2]

2.2 THE LEGISLATIVE SENTENCE: GEORGE COODE'S ANALYSIS

Every analysis of the legislative sentence has to begin with the exposition made by an English barrister named George Coode. In his exposition, the expression of every law essentially consists of, first, the description of the legal subject and, second, the enunciation of the legal action. Where the law is not of universal application two more elements are added. They are the description of the case to which the legal action is confined, the third; and, fourth, the conditions on performance of which the legal action operates.[3]

To paraphrase, according to Coode, every legislative sentence must have four elements, namely, the case, the condition, the legal subject, and the legal action to be taken. The following example should suffice to illustrate the analysis:

(a) Where a meeting of the Commission is called (case)

(b) and fifteen minutes elapse from the time set for the meeting (condition)

(c) the secretary (legal subject)

(d) shall abort the meeting (legal action).[4]

Loosely speaking, the legal subject is the grammatical subject and the legal action is the predicate. The "case" refers to the circumstances to which the law applies, while the "condition" refers to something that must be done for the law to operate.

This formula is used in many legal compositions, and the drafter must try to draft according to its precepts. However, as various authors have pointed out, not every legislative sentence, good or bad, can fit into this analysis. Whereas Coode's analysis remains a useful contribution to the syntax of many a legislative sentence, he has been rightly criticized for asserting that every legislative sentence is or has to be so constructed. In this regard, Thornton has said: "In cases of multiple and complex modification no absolute rules are possible".[5] In other words, as one tries to achieve clarity – that is, tries to apply the suggestions in this book – it will often be found that for clarity to be achieved a sentence has to be constructed outside of Coode's pattern. However, as much as possible, the case and condition, or the circumstances in which the law is called to operate, must appear first in a sentence and are often introduced by "where", "when" or "if".

Some legislative sentences are too short or have too few elements to fit within Coode's formula. For example, the sentence "The Director is the chief executive officer of the Commission" does not have all the elements Coode identified. Neither does the provision:

The functions of the Commission shall be to

(a) supervise the mutual funds industry; and

(b) do all other things necessarily incidental to the performance of the function in paragraph (a).

Even where the elements are technically present, that may be so only by reference. For example:

Where the conditions set out in subsection (5) are not satisfied, the Minister shall not issue a licence under this section but may issue a licence of the type prescribed under section 9.

However, even in constructing a provision that may only refer rather than set out the elements in full, Coode's analysis is still of some use.

2.3 AMENDMENTS

There are two principal forms of amendment: direct and indirect.[6] The distinction between direct amendment and indirect amendment is well known among drafters. A direct (or textual) amendment is one that clearly sets out how the principal law – that is, the one to be amended – is to be changed. For example, an amending Act may delete a figure from the principal Act and replace it with a different figure. In other cases a subparagraph, paragraph, subsection or section may be repealed and replaced by a re-crafted provision that may repeat some of the content of the old law. And as may be expected, where a provision calls for too many changes it is better to repeal the whole subparagraph, paragraph, subsection, section or Part or even the whole Act and replace it with a "new" provision or set of provisions.

Indirect amendments are those which do not literally state exactly how the law being amended will be affected. For example, a provision in an Occupational Health and Safety Act, 2007, may state:

> The power contained in section 7 to the Employment Act, 2000 to appoint inspectors is deemed to include a power to appoint inspectors for the purposes of health and safety.

Although it is possible to reconstruct section 7 to include the power being referred to, this section of the Occupational Health and Safety Act does not state exactly which words of section 7 of the Employment Act are to be affected and how.

Indirect amendments often present textual and citation problems, not to mention substantive problems. Textual problems arise in the following example taken from the British Virgin Islands. The Constitution was contained in the Virgin Islands (Constitution) Order, 1976, UKSI

2145 of 1976. Section 2 of the Virgin Islands (Constitution) (Amendment) Order 2000, UK SI 1343, had the following amendment:

2.– (1) Section 2 of the Constitution shall be amended by replacing subsection (2) by the following: –

"(2) For the purposes of this Order a person shall be deemed to belong to the Virgin Islands if that person –

(a) is born in the Virgin Islands and at the time of the birth his father or mother is –

(i) a British Dependent Territories citizen by virtue of birth, registration or naturalization in the Virgin Islands or by virtue of descent from a father or mother who was born in the Virgin Islands; or

(ii) settled in the Virgin Islands; and for this purpose "settled" means ordinarily resident in the Virgin Islands without being subject under the law in force in the Virgin Islands to any restriction on the period for which he may remain; or

(b) is born in the Virgin Islands of a father or mother who is deemed to belong to the Virgin Islands by birth or descent or who, if deceased, would, if alive, be deemed so to belong to the Virgin Islands; or

(c) is a child adopted in the Virgin Islands by a person who is deemed to belong to the Virgin Islands by birth or descent; or

(d) is born outside the Virgin Islands of a father or mother who is a British Dependent Territories citizen by virtue of birth in the Virgin Islands; or

(e) is a British Dependent Territories citizen by virtue of naturalization in the Virgin Islands; or

(f) is a person to whom a certificate has been granted under section 16 of the Immigration and Passport Act 1977 of the Virgin Islands (in this subsection referred to as "the Act", and references to the Act or to any section thereof include references to any enactment amending, replacing or re-enacting the same) and has not been revoked under section 17 of the Act; or

(g) is a spouse of a person deemed to belong to the Virgin Islands and has been granted a certificate under section 16 of the Act."

(2) For the purposes of the Constitution as amended by this Order, a person shall also be deemed to belong to the Virgin Islands if, immediately before the date on which this section comes into force, that person was deemed to belong to the Virgin Islands by virtue of section 2 (2) of the Virgin Islands (Constitution) Order 1976:

Provided that a person who was deemed to belong to the Virgin Islands by virtue of section 2 (2) (e) of that Order and who subsequent to attaining the age of twenty-one years is ordinarily resident outside the Virgin Islands for a period of not less than five years shall cease to be deemed to belong to the Virgin Islands.

When the time came to consolidate the constitution, meaning to reprint it incorporating all amendments, there was a textual problem, which a drafter will readily recognize. Subsection (2) of section 2 was deleted and replaced by the new subsection (2), the first one appearing in this provision, which is at the beginning of the whole provision. Thus everything from (a) up to (g) replaced what was there before. It will be noticed that at the end of (g) the quotation marks close off the whole of (2). However, there is a problem with the second (2), appearing immediately thereafter in the provision. This is subsection (2) to the amending Order and not subsection (2) to the principal Order. This second subsection (2), together with its proviso, belongs to the amendment Order only. It is not stated in the amendment Order that it should go into the principal Order. One of the things that the person consolidating it might do is reproduce the subsection, perhaps in a footnote, and next to it explain its effect. This is undesirable as it is slightly confusing. By drafting a direct amendment, the problem would have been avoided. The Virgin Islands Constitution Order 2007, UKSI 1678, corrected this anomaly.

The other problem has to do with the inconvenience of citation. Because each indirect amendment is technically an Act on its own, it has to continue to exist on its own and must always be cited separately – another point a drafter will readily discern. This may need illustration.

In many jurisdictions there exists the commendable practice of preparing only direct amendments. Zambia is one of many examples. There, an amending Act will, as a rule, state, for example: "This Act may be cited as the Income Tax (Amendment) Act 2003 and shall be read as one with the Income Tax Act, 2000, hereinafter referred to as the principal Act." By stating that the amendment Act is one with the principal Act, the amendment is, so to speak, self-effacing. Thus, for example, a lawyer in court who cites an amended section without citing the amendment will technically be correct. To put it another way, if section 4 of the amending Act changed a detail in section 7 of the Income Tax Act, such as the percentage of customs duty on motor vehicles from 2 per cent to 6 per cent, one may still, and rightly, state that the 6 per cent rate of tax is specified in section 7 of the Income Tax Act, 2000 – that is, the original Act – without, in strict law, having to refer to section 4 of the Income Tax (Amendment) Act, 2003.

It would, however, be informative for our lawyer to state in his citation that he is referring to section 7 of the Income Tax Act – as amended by section 4 of the Income Tax (Amendment) Act, 2001 – just in case a judge may be looking at the principal Act and is unaware of the amendment. Sometimes it is suggested that where a section that is being amended was amended before – for example, by an Income Tax (Amendment) Act, 2001, especially if the 2003 amendment relates to the same section and detail – the amending section must state that "section 7 of the principal Act (as amended by section 3 of the Income Tax (Amendment) Act) is amended by . . .".

Whereas parenthetic material stating that a section has been amended may be convenient in certain individual cases, it is not to be recommended as a general practice. If such material is to be used at all, it must be used consistently. That way if the parentheses are not used, the reader can assume that the section has not been amended since the last revision of the law or since enactment. Indeed, if such a practice were to be adopted, it would present citation problems of its own.

The incorporation of an amendment into the principal Act is not only textual but goes also to interpretation. The Interpretation Act, [Zam], section 16, expresses the generally accepted principle, "Where one written law amends another written law, the amending law shall, so far as it is consistent with the tenor thereof, be construed as one with the amended written law." Thus, for example, if a term is defined in the principal law, it will have the same meaning when used in the amending law unless it is clear, expressly or by necessary implication, that it is intended to be used with a different meaning.

When drafting an amendment Act, there are at least two ways of referring to the principal Act. One way is to refer to it in the very first section. For example,

> This Act may be cited as the Roads (Amendment) Act, 2001 and shall be read as one with the Roads Act (hereinafter referred to as "the principal Act").

Another way is exemplified by the following:

1. This may be cited as the Roads (Amendment) Act, 2001.

2. Section 8 of the Roads Act (hereinafter referred to as "the principal Act") is amended by deleting "person" and inserting in its place "officer".

3. Section 11 of the principal Act is amended by repealing subsection (5).

This latter practice is not recommended. First, the fact that an amendment Act amends, and will be read as part of, the principal Act, merits appearing in the same section that introduces the amendment Act. As much as this is a trite principle of interpretation, the average user of the law, who will seek to know straightaway what Act is being amended, will expect to find this information in the first section. He will not expect to find it in the second section or in a section that is also amending section 8, as above, or as the case may be.

Second, from a drafting perspective the practice can be inconvenient. Going further with our amendment that starts in section 2 by amending section 8 of the principal Act, at some point during the drafting process one may find that, for example, section 6 also needs amendment. Under the practice which cites the reference to the principal Act in the second section (in this case amending section 8) one will have to delete reference to the principal Act in section 2 and move that segment to the new section 2, which will be amending section 6.

Having already drafted the Bill on the lines shown above, he will be forced to delete in section 2 any reference to (what is in effect) the definition of "principal Act" and also renumber the clauses thus:

1. This may be cited as the Roads (Amendment) Act, 2001.

2. Section 6 of the Roads Act (hereinafter referred to as "the principal Act") is amended in subsection (4) by adding "by implication" at the end of the subsection.

3. Section 8 is amended by deleting "person" and inserting in its place "officer".

4. Section 11 of the principal Act is amended by repealing subsection (5).

It is enough of a nuisance to renumber the clauses. It is a double nuisance to have to move the definition of "the principal Act". Indeed, if a large Act is being amended and more sections in the earlier part of the amending Act are being added, the words may have to be moved more than once.

Also, as fate sometimes has it, the drafter may insert a new lead section, so to speak, after the citation and forget to delete the reference to the principal Act from what will now be section 3. Proofreading may, of course, take care of that. However, any practice must be deprecated that may or is likely to breed one or more possible errors. What is more, where the amending Act amends only one section, again under the second practice, you have to remember not to have the "hereinafter" clause in clause 2. This is because in that case clause 2 will just refer, in our example, to the Roads Act and will not have the hereinafter clause as it will be unnecessary. For all these reasons it is far easier to employ the first practice. That way, all the sections after section 1 will materially read the same, regardless of the number of sections being amended and regardless of whether new sections are inserted to amend new sections or, for that matter, whether a section that is touched in the first or subsequent draft is, in the end, amended.

There are a number of statutory rules that must be followed or taken into account when one is drafting amendments; this has been alluded to above. A citation of, or reference to, an enactment is deemed to be a citation of, or reference to, the enactment as amended. The provision in New Zealand states: "An amending enactment is part of the enactment it amends."[7] This provision technically applies to both Acts and regulations as "enactment" is so defined.[8]

The Interpretation Act, Cap. 2, [Zam], makes it clear in section 12 that:

> Where any written law which has been amended by any other written law is itself repealed, such repeal shall include the repeal of all those provisions of other written laws by which such first-mentioned written law has been amended.

In other words, if the Public Health Act is amended by the Public Health (Amendment) Act and other amendments, when a law called Public Health (Repeal) Act is passed, it is understood to be repealing all the amendments that were ever made to the Public Health Act. It is therefore not necessary to repeal the amending Acts specifically. No attempt should ever be made to do so. If the attempt is made, there is a danger that those that are not repealed will be considered to have been saved by implication, to the extent that they can stand alone.

The Acts Interpretation Act 1901, [Aus], section 14A, deals with the placing of definitions in amendments. It stipulates:

> Where an amending Act inserts a definition in a provision of the Act being amended, but does not specify the position in that provision where it is to be inserted, it shall be deemed to be inserted in the appropriate alphabetical position, determined on a letter-by-letter basis.

Some jurisdictions do not have this kind of provision. This makes it necessary, whenever a definition is being placed, to state, for example, that "The principal Act is amended by the insertion in its appropriate alphabetical place of the following definition:" or words to that effect.

The use of marginal notes[9] in relation to amendments presents its own considerations. In some jurisdictions, there is no arrangement of sections for an amendment Act. This would generally be because such an arrangement would not be very informative. In those jurisdictions where one is used, it would read, for example:

1. Short title

2. Amendment of section 2

3. Repeal and substitution of section 4

4. Repeal of section 9

Without an indication of the subject matter of the provision being amended, the reader may find that an indication of the sections affected is not of much use to him. Admittedly, if he is looking to see if a particular section has been amended, he may find it to be a useful start in his inquiry. In some cases, however, the inquirer is not looking for such information. He is more interested in the substance. For example, he may be looking to see if the Act deals with "Accounts and audit", "Disqualification from membership", "Dissolution of the corporation" and so on.

To deal with this problem, some jurisdictions have an arrangement of sections which is also substantively informative. Amendments are written in such a way that, in addition to an indication of the sections that are being amended or repealed, the subject matters of the provisions being amended or inserted are also indicated. For example, the arrangement of sections may read:

1. Short title and commencement

2. Amendment of section 2 – Interpretation

3. Amendment of section 4 – Composition of Board

4. Repeal and substitution of section 8 – Finance

5. Insertion of section 42A – Lodging of appeals

6. Insertion of sections 69A and 69B – Withdrawal of appeals; Success of appeals

There are, of course, a lot of issues that could be raised in relation to the system. In sections 2, 3 and 4 of the amendment Act, the substantive indication is from the existing marginal notes of sections 2, 4 and 8 of the principal Act. For purposes of this example, let us assume that sections 2 and 3 do not amend marginal notes. Let us also assume that section 4 of the amendment Act, the repeal and substitution, involves a change of the marginal note from "Finance" to "Financial obligations". You will notice that the new marginal note does not appear in the arrangement of sections. In section 5, which is inserting a whole new section, the indication is of the marginal note being assigned (for the first time since it is a new section) to that section. In relation to section 6, it is possible to indicate the marginal notes to the sections being amended in the manner shown. If the sections being inserted are too many, a generalization may be crafted. If no fair generalization can be made, one may just state "Insertion of new sections".

Also, it is worth keeping in mind the following. Amendments are difficult enough to understand at the best of times. Small additions, insertions and other changes usually present some inconvenience. The drafter must not compound these problems. He must try to ensure that such changes are as self-contained as possible. Here are a few examples. An amendment which says "ten" should be deleted and "seven" substituted therefor is not very informative at a glance. But the meaning of an amendment which says "ten days" is deleted and "seven days" substituted therefor is much easier to understand readily, for the reader knows right away that it is the number of days that has been changed.

On the whole, in some jurisdictions the presentation of amendments as a whole has changed. The once popular formulation "The principal Law is amended . . ." – and associated language – has been replaced with simpler, less verbose layouts. The following extract is from the Human Rights Amendment Act 2008, [ACT]:

1 Name of Act

This Act is the Human Rights Amendment Act 2008.

2 Commencement

(1) Sections 7, 8 and 9 commence on 1 January 2009.

(2) The remaining provisions commence on the day after this Act's notification day.

3 Legislation amended

This Act amends the Human Rights Act 2004.

4 Human rights may be limited
New section 28 (2)

insert

(2) In deciding whether a limit is reasonable, all relevant factors must be considered, including the following:

(a) the nature of the right affected;

(b) the importance of the purpose of the limitation;

(c) the nature and extent of the limitation;

(d) relationship between the limitation and its purpose;

(e) any less restrictive means reasonably available to achieve the purpose the limitation seeks to achieve.

5 Section 30

substitute

30 Interpretation of laws and human rights

So far as it is possible to do so consistently with its purpose, a Territory law must be interpreted in a way that is compatible with human rights.[10]

2.4 AVOIDING AMBIGUITY

2.4.1 SOME BASIC DRAFTING RULES

2.4.1.1 DRAFT IN THE SINGULAR

All legislation must be drafted in the singular unless the substance of the provision concerned calls for the plural to be used. First, it is easier to deal with the singular. Second, and more importantly, it avoids ambiguity in certain contexts. For example, the provision "Married persons shall not be in singles bars" does not make it clear whether this provision is violated only by a couple attending together or whether one-half of a couple can violate it on his or her own. If the former is intended, it may be rewritten "Married persons shall not together be in a singles bar." If the latter is the real rule, one may say "A married person shall not be in a singles bar." In this case, the rule will be violated not only where a single person goes into such a bar alone but also where a couple go together. In the latter case, of course, each will be in violation individually.

In the following provision from the Criminal Code, 1997 (of the British Virgin Islands), which is the usual way of stating the doctrine of common purpose, the plural is unavoidable:

> 20. When two or more persons form an intention to prosecute an unlawful purpose in conjunction with one another and in the prosecution of such unlawful purpose an offence is committed of such a nature that its commission was a probable consequence of the prosecution of such unlawful purpose, each of them is deemed to have committed the offence.

In this provision, also note the use of the expression "each of them" rather than "all of them".

It must also be observed that legislation usually provides for the matter of number. The Interpretation Act, Chapter 1-21, [Can], section

33 (2), exemplifies a common provision: "Words in the singular include the plural, and words in the plural include the singular."[11]

That means that if a law states that "The registered owner of a house may apply to have his house demolished at the expense of the State", it means that if there is more than one registered owner, the two or more registered owners may jointly make the application. This applies also in a case where the plural term is not a grammatical derivative of the singular term. Thus is has been held that where a statute made the act or omission of a "Minister" subject to judicial review, the act or omission of the Cabinet was also subject to judicial review by virtue of an Interpretation Act whereby "words in the singular shall include the plural".[12]

2.4.1.2 USE THE SAME WORD OR EXPRESSION FOR THE SAME THING

There is an approach to the interpretation of statutes that essentially states that it is assumed, unless the context requires otherwise, that a word or expression is used in the same sense throughout one piece of legislation. Conversely, where a different word or expression is used, it will be assumed, unless the context again dictates otherwise, that a different meaning was intended. This rule is also followed in drafting legislation and other legal instruments. There is no room for the elegant variation so beloved by novelists and other similar writers. Indeed, even where it appears that there may be no problem of interpretation, the rule must still be followed, as one can never be sure what a court will finally make of the provision after two well-paid competent counsel are done with trying to have it construed in accordance with what suits their respective clients. Further, it is not worth Parliamentary Counsel's time to try to argue whether the meaning would be the same. It is more practical just to stick to the rule.

2.4.1.3 CONFER A POWER OR IMPOSE A DUTY BY ACTIVE VOICE

The passive voice should be avoided wherever possible. The reason is that when it is used, one may not see that the provision does not confer a power or impose a duty on a specified person or authority. In the provision "A notice of meeting shall be served by registered post", it is not clear who has the duty unless there is some other provision that makes it clear whose duty this will be specifically or a provision that is wide enough to cover this duty. Even if there is such a provision, it may be poor communication, depending on circumstances. If one rewrites the provision in the active voice, it becomes imperative to identify who has the duty to serve the notice, as in "The company secretary shall serve a notice of meeting by registered post." And by the way, note that there is a surviving problem in that the reverse implication may be that some official other than the company secretary can serve a notice by post that is not registered.

2.4.2 PROBLEMATIC WORDS

2.4.2.1 "FROM" AND "TO"; "COMMENCING" AND "ENDING"

The word "from" can cause ambiguity. In a provision that states "A notice of change of directors shall be filed with the Registrar of Companies seven days from the date when the change takes place" it can be unclear whether the count begins on the day when the change takes place or whether it begins the day after. In favour of the latter interpretation, one may argue that the first day is not complete until twenty-four hours have elapsed from the time of the change, or that one day is not up, at the very least, until one moves from one day to the next. Similar problems are presented by the use of the term "commencing" as in "commencing on 8 June". Is 8 June to be counted as a full day?

At the other end of the spectrum, the words "to" and "ending" also can cause problems. Is the last named day to be counted or not, or does the period really end on the day before the last one named? When one says that someone's leave comes to an end on a certain day, does it mean that that day is the last day of leave or the first day of work? When the problem is realized, it is often easy to clarify the matter by simply stating on what date one returns to work or what the last day of leave is. The broader issue of computation of time is dealt with in more detail in item 2.4.4.2.

2.4.2.2 "Above" and "below"; "over" and "under"

These words present a problem that is similar to the problem in 2.4.2.1. The item that follows, 2.4.2.3, as well as item 2.4.4.2, will further elucidate the point with examples. All that needs to be stated here is that, generally speaking, to say "A child who is above 6 years old shall pay an admission fee of $8 and a child who is below 6 shall pay $2" leaves 6-year-olds uncatered for. The same applies to "over" and "under".

2.4.2.3 "Less than" and "more than"; "not exceeding" and "exceeding"

The expressions "less than" and "more than" make it clear that the number, date, weight or other similar thing mentioned is not covered. Instead of this pair of expressions, one should use "not exceeding" and "exceeding". In the following examples of a tax table, the first list leaves out certain incomes. The second covers all incomes:

Where a person's cumulative income

(a) is less than $3,000, 1 per cent;

(b) is more than $3,000 but less than $6,000, 5 per cent;

(c) is more than $6,000 but less than $12,000, 10 per cent.

Under that provision, if your cumulative income is exactly $ 3,000 or $6,000, there is no tax rate for you. This needs to be rewritten as follows:

Where a person's cumulative income

(a) does not exceed $3,000, 1 per cent;

(b) exceeds $3,000 but does not exceed $6,000, 5 per cent;

(b) exceeds $6,000 but does not exceed $12,000, 10 per cent.

Sometimes an attempt to deal with the problem in a different way proves unsatisfactory. The following does not eliminate the problem:

Where a person's cumulative income

(a) is up to $3,000, 1 per cent;

(b) is from $3,001 to $6,000, 5 per cent;

(c) is from $6,001 up to $12,000, 10 per cent.

The problem here, of course, is that if your income exceeds $3,000 by a cent or any figure up to 99 cents, you apparently do not have to pay tax. The same applies to cases where one's income exceeds $6,000 by similar amounts. Small errors like this breed litigation, requests for legal opinions and other kinds of inconvenience.

Such drafting errors are surprisingly common in legislation. The following example is from actual legislation in one jurisdiction:[13]

25. Subject to the provisions of sections 26 and 27, the tax payable under the provisions of section 5 shall be charged at the following rates:

INCOME	PERCENTAGE TAX
(a) From $1 to $3,000	0
(b) From $3,001 to $7,500	6
(c) From $7,501 to $15,000	10
(d) From $15,001 to $22,000	15
(e) Above $22,001	20

2.4.2.4 "Despite", "notwithstanding" and "subject to"

These expressions are used where two provisions would be in conflict with each other.[14] Generally speaking, an attempt must be made to identify the provision that overrides or that is to be overridden, as the case may be. This allows the reader to know readily what the law in that area is. In some cases, it is not practicable to specifically identify the provision. For example, imagine that there are in one jurisdiction a number of pieces of legislation dealing respectively with mutual funds, banks, trust companies and other kinds of financial institutions. Imagine also that each of these bodies is supervised by a different authority, and a decision is taken to bring them all under one umbrella body, which will register them and otherwise supervise them, called the Financial Services Commission. It is, of course, possible to amend all the relevant pieces of legislation to delete the former authority and replace it with the new body.

The obvious problem is that there are likely to be a number of other pieces of related legislation that refer to the old regulatory authorities, which may be called the Mutual Funds Commission, Banks and Trust Companies Commission and so on. Some of these references may not even be in the main legislation dealing with the particular type of financial institution but may be in amendments and other laws. Even after effecting the individual amendments to cater for the new body, it will still be necessary, out of abundance of caution, to stipulate something like "Notwithstanding any other law to the contrary, financial institutions shall be registered and supervised by the Financial Services Commission", assuming of course that "financial services" is defined.

Thornton has pointed out that it is not permissible to use the form "Subject to the provisions of any law to the contrary." He further states:

> This phrase suggests that there is in fact some law or laws to the contrary and creates a sense of insecurity in the mind of any person intending to act on the section. The reader is given no guidance regarding the real application of the provision.[15]

Further, it is circular in two coordinate provisions to use "notwithstanding" or "despite" in one and then use "subject to" in the other. The illogicality would go on without end. Imagine that there is a section in a Health Tax Act that says:

> 3. An organization that is profit-making in nature shall pay a health tax of 1% of its net profit.

Another section in the same Act may state:

> 8. Notwithstanding section 3 of this Act, the Minister may, in his discretion, exempt an organization from paying the health tax.

By the use in section 8 of the expression "notwithstanding", section 3 can be overridden by the minister. The word "despite" may also be used to the same effect.

Another way to achieve the same result is to state in section 3 that "Subject to section 8, an organization that is profit-making in nature shall pay . . .". If this is done, section 8 should not have the words "Notwithstanding section 3, . . .", for a section that has already subordinated itself to another section does not have to be overridden.

Before using the expression "subject to" the drafter must explore the possibility of achieving clarity by a more substantive statement in the section where he intends to use the words. In our example, the expression "subject to" can often be avoided by stating "An organization that is profit-making in nature shall pay a health tax of 1% of its net profit, unless it has been exempted under section 8" or "Except where the power in section 8 has been exercised . . .".

The use of "subject to" can cause even more serious problems. Consider the following provision:

> The President may constitute such offices for the Republic as he
> thinks fit and, subject to any law in force in the Republic, may
> make appointments to any such office.

Clearly, under this provision the words "subject to any law in force" will apply to procedural requirements that may be contained in a law. In other words, having constituted the offices, the President has to follow any procedures that may be prescribed to effect appointments. For example, the law may provide that he makes appointments by Gazette notice. However, does it also mean that once the President has made the law to constitute the offices, a law may be made to empower someone else to appoint persons to those offices? That is not very clear. The chances are that the latter was not the intention. The matter would have been put beyond doubt by stating clearly that the exercise of the power to appoint would be "subject to procedural requirements that may be prescribed by law". This is yet another illustration of the reason for the recommendation that "subject to" should not be used as a blunderbuss qualification. The kind of qualification must be identified and stated clearly.

2.4.2.5 "And" and "or"

Generally speaking, "and" is conjunctive while "or" is disjunctive. Some Interpretation Acts specifically state this. But as Thornton has pointed out, there can be overlap in meaning. He gives two examples and explains:

(1) A and B may do X.

(2) A or B may do X.

Example (1) conveys three possible meanings-

(i) A and B jointly may do X.

(ii) A may do X, B may do X or both A and B jointly may do X.

(iii) The single concept of A and B may do X (for example, if A = woman and B = doctor then a woman doctor may do X).

Example (2) means –

(i) Either A or B may do X, but not both of them.

(ii) A may do X, B may do X or both A and B may do X.

Thornton finally points out that meaning 1 (ii) and meaning 2 (ii) coincide and that "the matter is vaguely one of emphasis".[16]

Put simply, if a provision enumerates items and the connective "and" is used, it means that all the elements must be fulfilled. When "or" is used, it means that the satisfying of only one element is enough. This is the case where the connective is placed after each element or after only the penultimate element. Consider, for example, the provision:

No person shall be admitted to the club unless he is

(a) a member of the club;

(b) a guest of a member;

(c) a member of a sister club; or

(d) a guest of a member of a sister club.

In any provision that is set out in this way, placing an "or" or an "and" after item (c) only has the same effect as placing the connective repeatedly, that is, after (a), (b) and (c) as in the following:

No person shall be admitted to the club unless he is

(a) a member of the club; or

(b) a guest of a member; or

(c) a member of a sister club; or

(d) a guest of a member of a sister club.

In fact, in the above two examples, the connective is not necessary at all, as the nature of the categories is that they are likely to be mutually exclusive.

In some cases, it is necessary to use one or other of the connectives.

In the following provision, the connective "and" is in a sense needed:

An application for a licence must contain the following:

(i) Name;

(ii) Residential address;

(iii) Postal address;

(iv) Place of business; and

(v) Proposed date for commencement of business.

If a connective were left out, one may assume that all the elements must be stated, but that would be only because logic would so dictate. On the other hand, if the connective "or" were used after the first four elements or after only the penultimate element, then, strictly speaking, an application that contains only one of the five elements would be in compliance with the provision. This is an example of a case where, if by inadvertence an "or" were to be used, a court would be forced to bail out the drafter and hold that "or" means "and".

Also, an enumeration of definitions does not need either "and" or "or", as in the following:

In this Act, unless the context otherwise requires,
"food" includes potable water;
"engineer" includes a technician or technologist;
"police officer" means a full-time or auxiliary police officer.

There is no need in the foregoing itemization of definitions to place "and" before the penultimate definition or, for that matter, at the end of the first two definitions. There is no loss of meaning and, indeed, any such connective must be discouraged as superfluous.

The same goes for regulation-making power unless it is complex. In the following example from section 25 of the Bees Act [Ont], there was no need for a connective:

The Lieutenant Governor in Council may make regulations,

(a) prescribing the fees that shall be paid for a certificate of registration;

  . . .

(g) designating any disease of bees to be a disease within the meaning of this Act;

(h) designating any insect or parasite to be a pest within the meaning of this Act;

(i) prescribing forms and providing for their use.[17]

However, care must be taken in relation to elements of the enumerated powers where under that one element, there is a further enumeration. The following is an example from section 12(1) of the Charitable Institutions Act [Ont]:

The Lieutenant Governor in Council may make regulations,

(a) exempting designated approved corporations or charitable institutions from specified provisions of the Act or the regulations;

  . . .

(r) instituting a system for reconciling the payments made by the Crown under section 9 on account of the maintenance and operating costs of an approved charitable home for the aged with the actual maintenance and operating costs of the home, including,

  (i) requiring the approved corporation to provide, at specified intervals, audited financial statements, proof of maintenance and operating costs, information about the level of occupancy of the home and other documents and information,

    (ii) requiring that the information provided by the approved corporation for the purpose of reconciliation be provided under oath, and

    (iii) providing for the recovery by the Crown of any excess payment through deduction from subsequent payments to the approved corporation;

(s) prescribing the extraordinary events in respect of which the Minister may make additional grants to an approved corporation under section 9.1;

    . . .¹⁸

Clearly if regulations are to be made under paragraph (r), they must provide for all the three sub-elements. Of course there will be circumstances where, in a similar context, "or" would be the appropriate connective. It is recommended that where a connective is used, it is used after each element or sub-element. It is easier for all categories of readers to understand.

2.4.2.6 "SHALL", "MAY" AND "MUST"

The expression "shall" denotes obligation, whereas "may" is an empowering word. Generally in legislation "may" does not mean "might". Some statutes have legislated to that effect. For example, the Interpretation Act, Chapter 1-21, [Can], makes it clear. It states:

11. The expression "shall" is to be construed as imperative and the expression "may" is permissive.

In old drafts, one sometimes encounters a provision such as "If the tenant shall violate this provision . . .". In modern times, this is generally regarded as incorrect usage at worst and unduly stilted at best. It is better written as "If a tenant violates . . .".

It is often said that "shall" can mean "may" and "may" can mean "shall". It should suffice to say, as alluded to above, that courts have been forced into these constructions by what essentially was a failure to conceptualize adequately in relation to the connective. Consider, for example, the following provision:

> Where the licensing authority refuses to issue a licence, the applicant may appeal to the minister, who may render a final decision on the matter.

Faced with such a provision, a court will be compelled to construe the provision as imposing an obligation on the minister to make a decision. That is because it does not make sense to give a right of appeal and then go on to state that the minister is not obliged to consider and determine the appeal!

In some quarters "shall" has been sacrificed for "must" to impose an obligation. The Law Reform Commission of Victoria, in Australia, recommends the use of "must" to impose an obligation instead of "shall".[19] Thornton has also said that: "It is preferable to use 'must' instead of 'shall' to impose an obligation. This is more in line with ordinary speech and avoids the confusion that the use of 'shall' may introduce." [20] As Asprey has observed: "Both the Australian and the New South Wales Parliamentary Counsel's Offices also use must (or occasionally other expressions like is required to or is to) rather than shall, to impose an obligation or express a duty." [21] I make further observations in this regard in item 2.5.1 Verb tense.

2.4.2.7 "In accordance with"

Like "subject to", the expression "in accordance with" can refer to the substantive part of the provisions as well as the procedural part. It is important to keep that in mind. If the intention is merely, for example, to confer a right of appeal without also prescribing the procedure, the provision could read: "An appeal made under section 4 . . ." rather than "An appeal made in accordance with section 4 . . .". The latter should be used where the section contains only the procedure, or both the procedure and the substantive right to appeal. One reason for this distinction is that, where the provision merely confers a right of appeal (which may or may not be exercised), it is a false imperative to use the expression "in accordance with".

Consider the following example:

9. (1) A person who is aggrieved by a decision of a Magistrate in refusing to grant a restraining order may appeal to the High Court.

   (2) An appeal shall be made by the aggrieved person filing Form 5.

In referring to this provision, one may rightly say that the appeal is made under section 9 (1) but is filed in accordance with subsection (2). The appeal is not made in accordance with subsection (1), as that subsection does not contain an obligation to appeal. Subsection (2) contains an obligation for those who wish to appeal; therefore the expression "in accordance with" is apt.

2.4.3 CONTEXTUAL AMBIGUITY

Whereas a dictionary contains meanings of words, in practice the different meanings that a word is capable of bearing are often determined by context. For example, the word "bank" may mean different things to a person working in a financial institution and to a riparian dweller or river scientist. For a financial expert, "bank" will mean a commercial bank, development bank or other type of financial institution. For a person associated with rivers, the river bank may be the first thing he thinks of when he hears the word – although that may depend on whether he is downtown when he hears it and by whom it is mentioned.

Context is what clarifies these possible ambiguities. Drafters often resort to definitions to put things beyond doubt or to give special meanings to words or expressions.

2.4.4 AMBIGUITY IN GENERAL

Many a time a drafter sitting in a meeting has had someone point out to him what appears to be an ambiguity. Often, when he concedes this, some sharp cookie will argue, "No one can read it in that way! That would be unreasonable!" The problem, of course, is not always that simple. As is further explained in item 3.3.4, words are read in their entire context, both internal and external. A court will often, and justifiably, read a statute in a sense that is not the obvious one when one reads the statute at first instance. It will take the second, third or even subsequent meaning if that will create harmony in the statute or achieve its makers' purpose more efficaciously. Also, it must not be forgotten that when an apparently simple matter comes up for interpretation in a court of law, the stakes may be very high for the litigants. The losing party may suffer financially, socially or otherwise as a result of the court's finding. In the mix there will also be lawyers skilled in the art of reading a statute and formulating arguments that are aimed at convincing the court that their interpretation, though apparently unreasonable, is the better one – or at least the lesser of two evils. With or without good arguments before the court, there will be judges who will feel strongly one way or the other owing to their moral or professional orientation, or even out of personal sympathy for one of the parties as a result of what have been called inarticulate major premises. It is therefore very important that when even a slight ambiguity is detected, an attempt is made to address it and eliminate it.

There will be times when an ambiguity is pointed out and a lawyer states that there are rules of interpretation that resolve the ambiguity, and it is therefore not necessary to make it clearer than the rules of interpretation would render it. The problem is that even the rules of interpretation do not always give one signal. In physics there is a rule of natural science that for every motion there is an equal and opposing motion. So it is with rules of interpretation. For every rule there is almost always an equal and opposing rule. For example, there is the *ejusdem generis* rule, which states that general words at the end of an enumeration of things that fall into one clear and distinct class must be construed as being restricted to that class, regardless of how general the words might be. On the other hand, there is the golden rule, which obliges us to try to construe a law harmoniously so that one part of it is not brought into conflict with another. It should be easy to see how an attempt to apply the *ejusdem generis* rule may result in one provision of a statute being read in a way that brings it into conflict with another. Examples are given elsewhere in this book.[22]

One often encounters the argument that any further clarification of a provision is for the court to undertake. This position has its place and, applied to certain contexts, is inescapable. The practical problem the drafter faces is that it is sometimes applied to cases for which it is inappropriate. There will be cases where vagueness is useful so that a court, in the interests of justice, can apply a provision flexibly depending on circumstances. For example, rules of court often provide that if a document is not filed within a specified period, the court may allow it to be filed out of time, if that would be in the interests of justice. Such a provision may exist on its own or as an omnibus provision in addition to other specified grounds upon which lodgment out of time may be allowed. This type of vagueness is necessary because one cannot foresee all the circumstances that may make it right to allow late filing. Accordingly, it allows the court to dispense justice using its discretion from case to case.

There will also be cases where, for example, a licensing body is conferred authority not to issue a liquor licence for a reason such as that the applicant is below the age of 21, the applicant has a conviction relating to dishonesty, or it is not in the public interest. As vague as "public interest" is, it gives the court some basis on which to consider unforeseen circumstances. Admittedly, it can also open the door to abuse by authorities, but courts have developed principles to guide authorities and themselves on what is the meaning of "public interest". There are numerous other circumstances in which vagueness is desirable or understandable.

In some cases, it is unreasonable to leave the matter open and vague because it may cause injustice. For example, in legislation that deals with the (unpleasant) subject of detention without trial in a declared emergency, some jurisdictions provide that the grounds of detention must be served on the detainee within a specified number of days and the grounds must, without fail, be delivered within those days or the detention will be invalid. The same legislation may also provide that the grounds of detention must be "in detail" without defining the term. This, again, allows for modalities of application.

The call of the drafter is to discern which kinds of provisions require vagueness and which require clarity. A drafter must not shirk his responsibility to make a statute clear if there is no possible injustice that may occur if he does so, or where justice would positively require that the statute be clear, and where clarity is achievable from a drafting perspective. The fact that there is a rule of interpretation that is expected to make it clear is, on its own, not a good reason for leaving a statute vague.

I should add that when a court is considering a provision, it is faced with a fait accompli. The statute has been passed, and the court only has to interpret it. At the drafting stage, a drafter must not attempt to advance or entertain even good arguments as to why one interpretation is better than another. In some contexts he must be able to acknowledge that one interpretation is better than another but still concede, where a weaker but plausible interpretation can be made, the desirability of clarifying the matter further to ensure that the effect he is seeking is clearer. Courts deal with a garment that has been woven. They are therefore and to that extent in a bind. A drafter weaves the garment. He must not put himself in a difficult position unnecessarily.

In reading the segments on ambiguity that follow, it must be remembered that even when the illustrated ambiguities can resolve themselves, perhaps even easily, to an extent the drafter will have already failed if the matter gets to court at all. When he is drafting, it is inefficient to delve too much into rules of interpretation as justification for unduly loose expression. Accordingly, it is fairly standard advice that a drafter must know the rules of interpretation and draft with them in mind. His primary aim, however, is to make the draft as clear as possible, ensuring that no rule of interpretation will defeat the legislators' intention.

Cases also exist where an ambiguity is detected but there is no obvious way to resolve it without raising new issues. It may be that even where there is a way in which the issues can be dealt with, the drafter does not have the time to deal with them. Often in such circumstances, the drafter will suggest that although there is a plausible but clearly undesirable interpretation, the draft should be adopted without any change or further change. He may recommend that, owing to time constraints and assuming that a court is likely to adopt the better view, any possible misconstruction must be left to the rules of interpretation. When there is time, however, and the clarification is otherwise feasible, it must be effected unless change is likely to cause further problems.

2.4.4.1 Ambiguous modification

(a) Adjectives attached to a series

A common cause of ambiguity is the attachment of one or more adjectives to a series of nouns. Consider:

Only a respected lawyer or accountant may be appointed Chairperson of the Board.

Does the word "respected" apply only to "lawyer" and not to "accountant", meaning that a lawyer has to be of the respected kind but that an accountant can be an unprincipled scoundrel?

On the assumption that accountants are as much in need of respectability as lawyers, one way to correct this is to indent it:

A respected

(a) lawyer;

(b) accountant.

Of course, it can also be corrected to:

Only

(a) a lawyer,

(b) an accountant,

who is respected may be appointed Chairperson of the Board.

If the author intends to distinguish between the criterion applying to a lawyer and that applying (actually none) to an accountant, one might say:

Only

(a) a respected lawyer;

(b) an accountant;

may be appointed Chairman of the Board.

One may also formulate it like this:

Only a respected member of the following professions may be appointed Chairperson of the Board:

(a) law;

(b) accounting.

That formulation, however, may be unduly fragmented. An even better formulation may be:

Only a respected member of the law or accounting profession may be appointed Chairman of the Board.

Incidentally, notice that the expression "legal profession" is avoided, even if it is idiomatic, because accounting is also a profession that may be practised without breaking the law. For the same reason the expression "legal affairs officer" is to be preferred over "legal officer", despite the former being one word longer. For good measure, we may add that the expression "Foreign Minister" is clear only because of usage and because, in written form, it is often capitalized. Linguistically, a Minister of Health from country A being hosted in country B by his counterpart there is a foreign minister.

The adjective problem is also evident in the following:

a licensed surveyor or architect
an appointed Member of Parliament or Minister
a neatly arranged bouquet of flowers or books

Barring the most exotic of circumstances, the first of the examples above will be read to mean that "licensed" applies to both a surveyor and an architect. In the second example, though the formulation is one that may produce ambiguity, the subject matter itself does not render the provision ambiguous. Whereas in some systems some Members of Parliament may be appointed rather than elected, all ministers in any system are likely to be appointed. However, out of abundance of caution, it is still advisable to reformulate the provision as "a Minister or an appointed Member of Parliament".

The foregoing examples of adjective problems have to do with the connective "or". The problem also presents itself in cases where "and" is used, as in:

the green and white jerseys of Mufulira Wanderers

Are we talking here about striped or checked jerseys, or about two sets of jerseys, one solid green and the other solid white?

Here are a few more examples, these relating to the hereafter:

the late Mrs Moonga's sister
the Minister of Lands, then late Michael Hodge,

The problem with the first example is that it is unclear who is late, Mrs Moonga or her sister. The writer might have meant either "Mrs Moonga's late sister" or "the sister of the late Mrs Moonga". The second example is rather worse, especially with the use of the comma in the wrong place. It does for a moment suggest that Mr Hodge is no longer late. The writer must have meant "The Minister of Lands then, the late Michael Hodge," which would make it certain that he never came back from the other world.

The expression "the temporary employment agency" raises similar problems. A hyphen between the first two words means that the agency offers employment of the temporary kind, while a hyphen between the last two means that it is the employment agency itself which is temporary. In "wage earning employees", however, there is no need for a hyphen to clarify. Although it would be correct to insert a hyphen after "wage", it is not fatal if one is not used. In using compound nouns with adjectives, the writer must decide whether a hyphen is necessary. If in doubt, it is usually better to err on the side of clarity.

(b) Modifying verbs

Separating an auxiliary verb from the main verb was frowned upon and even forbidden by classical grammarians. One was not allowed to say:

> Where an employee commits any of the violations mentioned in this section, the Manager may, without notice, dismiss him.

or

> The Minister shall, where a member is absent without a reasonable explanation, revoke his appointment.

The verbs "may dismiss" and "shall revoke" were supposed to stay together, respectively. Similarly, problems can result from adhering to the "never split an infinitive" rule that used to be propounded by grammarians (it is falling out of favour, as it should). Ambiguity is sometimes created when adverbs such as "immediately" and "only" cannot be placed between "to" and the other part of an infinitive.

Here is an example of the ambiguity that results when a writer refuses to split two parts of a verb:

> When the Child Welfare Officer receives a complaint about the abuse of a child he shall instruct counsel to seek a restraining order immediately.

What is to be done immediately? Is it the instructing of counsel by the Child Welfare Officer or the seeking of a restraining order by the solicitor? The problem is that the writer has decided not to split the verbs "shall instruct" and "to seek".

Liberated from pedantic grammarianism, he could have formulated it as follows:

When the Child Welfare Officer receives a complaint about the abuse of a child, he shall immediately instruct counsel to seek a restraining order.

Common sense would, of course, dictate that once the instruction is given, the seeking of the order by counsel must also be done immediately, unless there is legal advice to the contrary. The splitting of the verb, however, makes it clear that it is the instructing that has to be done immediately. (Admittedly, the nature of the matter suggests that both the instructing and the seeking of an order should be done immediately.)

Reed Dickerson has made the point clearly:

However offensive it may be to many persons, the split infinitive makes clear beyond all doubt what the adverb modifies. The same is true of other split verb forms. There can be no doubt, for example, as to the meaning of "shall promptly require". The draftsman, therefore, should not hesitate to split an infinitive or other verb form if to do otherwise would create the significant possibility of ambiguity.[23]

Thornton is even more emphatic, stating that "descriptive works founded on usage instead of prescriptive theoretical niceties have done much to reduce the influence of such foolish rules".[24]

Consider, finally, the placement of the small but powerful word "only":

A senior player only may play after 6:00 PM.

Does this mean that all players, including senior ones, may play up to 6:00 PM, but only senior ones can continue to play after that time? Or does it mean that the senior players may not play before 6 PM but only after that time? This can be clarified by splitting the verb "may play":

A senior player may only play after 6:00 PM.

The word "only" can also be placed after the verb:

A senior player may play only after 6:00 PM.

(c) Phrases

A common and easily identifiable cause of ambiguity is a phrase following two substantive elements, such as:

a barrister or solicitor who has practised for at least two years
a soccer player or rugby player who is about to retire

Do the phrases beginning with "who" apply also to the barrister and to the soccer player? If they do not, the easiest way to clarify it is to switch the position of the first substantive, thus:

a solicitor who has practised for at least two years or a barrister
a rugby player who is about to retire or a soccer player

The following are common examples of careless wording that leads to ambiguity:

I saw him walking down the street.
An operator of a transport business in the Caribbean must be
    licensed.
No person may kick another player on a soccer pitch.
No person shall participate in the spraying of insecticide with-
    out a licence.
I saw the dog lying in the kennel.

Who was walking down the street, the person seeing or the person seen? Who is in the Caribbean, the operator or the business, or both?

In the third example, is the violation committed when both the person kicking and the person being kicked are on the pitch? If the kicker is on the pitch and the person being kicked is not on the pitch or the converse, is the violation still committed? As for the spraying of insecticide, it is not clear whether it is the person or the insecticide which needs to be licensed. In the final example, one would hope that it is the dog that was lying in the kennel and not the person seeing it!

One final example:

The police are looking for a suspect with one eye.

Why would the police be using only one eye to look for a suspect who may have two good eyes? Why don't they use all their eyes so that they have a better chance of catching the criminal?

(d) Clauses

These generally present the same type of problem as we saw with phrases:

- a coach who has coached a gymnast who has taken banned steroids
- a company which owns an aeroplane which is registered in Miami

In both formulations, it is not clear whether the second relative clauses relate also to the coach and the company, respectively. It must be admitted that it is probable that, in these examples, the clauses do not refer to the first antecedent as well as to the second. In everyday usage, such constructions are likely to be understood as referring to the immediately preceding antecedent. In a legal document, however, the cost of misconstruction can be high, and the argument that the relative clause refers to both may carry the day even if that was never the intention. Matters must be clarified as much as possible.

Also, in the sentence

No person shall, without informing the Director, dismiss a police officer, firefighter or soldier working for the federal government,

it is not clear whether "working for the federal government" applies to a police officer and firefighter as well as a soldier. If it applies only to the last of the three elements it would have been better written as:

No person shall, without informing the Director, dismiss a soldier working for the federal government, a police officer or a firefighter.

(e) Participles

In the following sentence, who or what is in an adulterated condition?

No person shall sell food in an adulterated condition.

On the assumption that persons cannot be in an adulterated condition, what was meant is:

No person shall sell food that is in an adulterated condition.

That would be slightly clearer, but better still, it should have said:

No person shall sell unwholesome food.

The additional point here is that sometimes rearranging the words is not sufficient to achieve clarity; the words themselves may have to be changed.

In the next example, it is not abundantly clear whether there are certain kinds of beer which have a mouth!

No person shall take part in the brewing of beer frothing at the mouth.

Then there is the following sentence, whose underlying assumption inventors are still working on:

No person shall carry on the planting of grain walking on foot.

When the grain is invented which can walk on foot, we will not need planters!

(f) Pronouns

Faulty pronominal reference is easy to detect and yet very common. It is sometimes said that pronouns must be avoided in legislation because of their ability to cause ambiguity. The better view is that pronouns must be used cautiously. Excessive repetition of the subject can create unduly awkward sentences. Regardless of the fact that it is more important for legal documents to be clear than to be elegant, elegance must not be destroyed by design under the guise of clarity. Let elegance be sacrificed to clarity only when necessary.

In the following sentence, to whom does "he" refer?

When the tenant has dispatched the cheque for the first month's rent and the landlord has received it, he shall register the lease.

It is unclear who has the obligation to register the lease. The easiest way to deal with the matter is to repeat the noun. Instead of "he", the word "landlord" or "tenant", depending on the intention, should be used.

(g) Ambiguity regarding nationality

Ambiguous references to nationality are often heard on television. For example, a coach of England's national soccer team can be described as "the English coach", and it causes no problems if he is an Englishman and the context is clear. If, on the other hand, he happens to be of another nationality, the term will be inapt. Then it becomes necessary to say "the England coach". We could also say, though it uses more words, "the coach of the English team".

2.4.4.2 DATE, AGE AND TIME

Date, age and time are usually considered in relation to the commencement of legislation and in measuring what we may call, subject to what is said below, periods of time. Legislation is often expressed to come into force on a particular day. For example, "This Act comes into operation on 10 June 2010."

Most Interpretation Acts make it clear that under such a provision the legislation concerned comes into effect on the expiration of the previous day.[25] Indeed, the Interpretation Act should always be consulted in regard to the commencement of legislation and in relation to the computation of time for the doing of anything under a law. Almost invariably, there will be provisions governing the matter.

The issue of date and time also often arises in relation to the word "between". There is, of course, no problem when one states that "Nomination papers shall be filed between 6:00 AM and 6:00 PM" on a named date. Where, however, a provision states that "Complaints shall be filed between Monday and Wednesday" this means, technically, that complaints can be filed only on Tuesdays. And if we state that "Complaints shall be filed between Monday and Tuesday", for all practical purposes, we state a nonsense.

In relation to age, further to what has been said in item 2.4.2.1, one must take care to use "between" carefully. A provision that states that

A person between the ages of 16 and 21 may marry only with the consent of both parents excludes the ages of 16 and 21. It means that if you are 16 you cannot marry, even if you have parental consent. Although one could draft a provision using "between" by design, understanding what it means, the formulation would still be objectionable on the basis that it gives prominence to numbers that are not the significant ones. Consider, for example, if the provision above had stated, in effect, that a person who has attained the age of 16 years but has not attained the age of 21 can marry but only with parental consent. One could use the expression "between" and achieve the same substantive result by saying:

> A person who is between the ages of 15 and 22 may marry only with the consent of both parents.

That would technically achieve the intended result but is objectionable on the basis that it gives prominence to the age of 15 when that age is not significant. The significant age is 16, and it must therefore be given prominence. The same is true for the age of 22. A better formulation is:

> A person who has attained the age of 16 years but has not attained the age of 21 may marry only with the consent of both parents.

The expression "more than 16 years of age" can also cause ambiguity. When children are born, their age or longevity on earth is thought of in terms of hours, days, weeks, months and years. Later in life, age is thought of largely in terms of years. Thus, when one states that "only a person who is more than 16 years of age can vote" this may be understood in terms of years, meaning that a person who is 16 but not yet 17 is not covered. In other words "more than 16 years" can be held to mean a person who is 17 years or older. Matters can be put beyond doubt by stating:

> Only a person who has passed his 16th birthday . . .

The same problem manifests itself in relation to the words "after" and "before". What has been said in relation to "between" generally applies also to these two words and other similar expressions.[26] The criticisms of using "between" by design, knowing its true meaning, apply here also.

There are also problems with the word "by" when used in expressions such as "Applications shall be filed by 21 May". It is unclear whether that is the last day on which applications may be filed. It is clearer to say "The last day for filing applications is 21 May."

I mentioned in item 2.4.2.1 how use of a word such as "from" in relation, for example, to the doing of an act leaves it unclear as to whether the first day is to be counted. Similarly, when a provision states that an appeal must be filed within fourteen days, it is unclear whether the day on which the decision is given is counted or partly counted. It is sometimes suggested that reference to "full days" would make it clear that the day on which the decision is made is not counted. But even this is not so clear, for if the court rendering the decision rises at 12:00 noon, having given the decision, it is arguable that at noon the following day a full day would have been completed, and so on. The best way to express it is the time-honoured expression "clear days". This means that the day on which the judgment is rendered is excluded.

Some of these and other problems are dealt with by the following provisions from the Interpretation Act, Chapter 1-21, [Can.]:

Computation of Time

26. (1) Where the time limited for the doing of a thing expires or falls on a holiday, the thing may be done on the day next following that is not a holiday.

R.S., 1985, c. 1-21, s. 26; 1999, c. 31, s. 147 (F)

27. (1) Where there is a reference to a number of clear days or "at least" a number of days between two events, in calculating

that number of days the day on which the first event happens is excluded and the day on which the second event happens is included.

(2) Where there is reference to a number of days, not expressed to be clear days, between two events, in calculating that number of days the day on which the first event happens is excluded and the day on which the second event happens is included.

(3) Where a time is expressed to begin or end at, on or with a specified day, the time includes that day.

(4) Where time is expressed to begin after or to be from a specified day, the time does not include that day.

(5) Where anything is to be done within a time after, from, of or before a specified day, the time does not include that day.

R.S., c. 1-23, s. 25

28. Where there is a reference to a period of time consisting of a number of months after or before a specified day, the period is calculated by

(a) counting forward or backward from the specified day the number of months, without including the month in which that day falls;

(b) excluding the specified day; and

(c) including in the last month counted under paragraph (a) the day that has the same calendar number as the specified day or, if that month has no day with that number, the last day of that month.

R.S., c. 1-23, s.25

29. Where there is a reference to time expressed as a time of the day, the time is taken to mean standard time.

R. S., c.1-23, s. 25

30. A person is deemed not to have attained a specified number of years of age until the commencement of the anniversary, of the same number, of the day of that person's birth.

R.S., c. 1-23, s. 25.[27]

The following is an example from the Interpretation Act, [Zam]:

GENERAL PROVISIONS RELATING TO TIME AND DISTANCE

35. In computing time for the purpose of any written law –

(a) a period of days from the happening of an event or the doing of any act or thing shall be deemed to be exclusive of the day on which the event happens or the act or thing is done;

(b) if the last day of the period is Sunday or a public holiday (which days are in this section referred to as "excluded days") the period shall include the next following day, not being an excluded day;

(c) where any act or proceeding is directed or allowed to be done or taken on a certain day, then, if that day happens to be an excluded day, the act or proceeding shall be considered as done or taken in the due time if it is done or taken on the next day afterwards, not being an excluded day;

(d) where an act or proceeding is directed or allowed to be done or taken within any time not exceeding six days, excluded days shall not be reckoned in the computation of the time.[28]

2.4.4.3 CLAUSES STARTING WITH "BECAUSE" AND "WITHOUT"

Careless use of these words can produce interesting ambiguity. For example:

> The Chairman presented the award and the author received it without saying anything.

Who did not say anything, the giver or the receiver, or both? If it was the Chairman, it should be rephrased:

> The Chairman, without saying anything, presented the award and the author received it.

Of course we do not know if the author, having received the award, said anything, but we could assume that he did, since the writer of the sentence mentioned only that the giver did not do so.

In the following sentence, it is not clear to what the relative clause refers.

> The Directors suspended players who did not want to play because they were against the policies of the government.

Did the directors suspend these players because of the reason the players advanced for not playing? Who was against the policies of the government? It is not clear to whom the pronoun "they" refers – the directors or the players.

2.4.4.4 OTHER ASPECTS OF AMBIGUITY: CROSS-REFERENCING

As much as possible, cross-references must be specific. Where the intention is to refer to a Part, section, subsection, paragraph, subparagraph or any other provision (other than the one being drafted), that other provision must be clearly identified. This makes the intention of the provision clear from the beginning. No matter how convinced the drafter is that a vague cross-reference is easy to decipher, he must not leave it up to the reader.

Accordingly, there are certain vague words that must be avoided. Vague references are often made with expressions such as "said", "aforesaid", "aforementioned" and "abovementioned". These are objectionable in the first place because they are archaic. We no longer meet an acquaintance on the street and say "Whither goest thou?" Why should we in writing continue using expressions that are equally awkward? Second, these words can be rendered non-specific by context. The following are examples of how they are sometimes used:

the said rate of tax

the aforesaid term of employment

the aforementioned building

the abovementioned code of conduct

If there is only one rate of tax, term of employment, building or code of conduct referred to, especially where the legislation is short, there may be no problem identifying the antecedent that is being referred to. However, it is easier on the reader if the drafter specifically refers to the provision in which the antecedent appears. If the antecedent is in the same provision, there may be no problem of ambiguity, but instead of an expression such as "the aforementioned rate of tax", it is better in many contexts to write "that rate of tax", and so on.

Consider the following:

Where the rate of tax payable under section 7 by the types of club listed in Schedule 1 is challenged on the basis that the club does not fall within that class, the assessment of tax based on the aforementioned rate shall be paid pending consideration of the appeal.

In the example, it is quite clear that the rate of tax being referred to is the rate specified in section 7. The dated air created by the word "aforementioned" can be eliminated by simply saying "that rate of tax".

The words "said", "aforesaid", "aforementioned" and "abovementioned" are problematic also because they can refer to any provision right up to the beginning of the legislation. It will always be unclear whether they are referring to the subparagraph, paragraph, subsection, section, Part or other heading.

Similar considerations apply to another group of words, at least in their quality of being uninformative. These are "following", "foregoing", "preceding" and "succeeding". Thornton has pointed out:

> These are also imprecise words of legislative reference; a more specific reference should be preferred. When used to indicate the position of other legislative provisions, their inadequacy is not cured by prefixing the adjectives "last" or "next" because of the possibility that the legislature may insert a new provision and thus make the reference erroneous.[29]

It is no answer to say that if there is an amendment, the drafter must deal appropriately with the change. It is too much effort to require of a drafter in a matter that could easily have been dealt with simply by making a more precise reference in the first place. Instead, drafting practices must ensure that, in the event an amendment is made later, there is little chance of an error being generated.

The words "above" and "below" are not very informative in some contexts. They can refer to all the provisions preceding or all the provisions following. In some statutes there is an attempt to deal with the point by stating:

The persons referred to in paragraph (e) below.

Here the word "below" becomes superfluous because the reference is clear without it. It is a matter of common sense that when a reference is made in a subsection to a specific paragraph, that has to be a paragraph in the particular subsection. In any case, many Interpretation Acts contain a provision which states that wherever in a written law there is reference to a subparagraph, paragraph or subsection, the reference shall be understood to be to a subparagraph, paragraph or subsection in the paragraph, subsection or section, respectively, in which the reference is found.

The words "herein", "hereinafter", "hereinbefore" and "heretofore" must be avoided. The first three, as we have observed in relation to similar words, do not clearly inform the reader whether the reference is to the subparagraph, paragraph, subsection, section, Part, other heading or the entire statute. Besides, they are archaic. Conveyancers often get away with "herein" but that is because of context. In a lease, for example, there is often a part where the obligations of the landlord are set out and another where those of the tenant are spelt out. Thus a reference such as "the obligations of the landlord herein referred to" will be reasonably clear so long as all the obligations are set out under that heading.

The word "hereinafter" deserves additional mention. Again, a comparison with conveyancing documents is useful. In a deed, this can be used at the very beginning of the document, often in relation to definitions. The deed will begin:

THIS DEED is made this   day of   BETWEEN
Bill Bond (hereinafter referred to as "the Buyer") and Bill Band
(hereinafter referred to as "the Seller").

Even if the word "hereinafter" is replaced with "herein", there is no problem of imprecision because it appears at the beginning of the document. The only surviving objection is the fact that the words are aged. In legislation, these circumstances cannot as easily or as frequently be replicated, and thus the admonition against them has to stand.

Further, in relation to "hereinafter" it is worth noting that the vagaries of drafting pose great danger. In the process of drafting, the drafter may introduce a new concept – for example, a definition – which he expects will only be used from a particular point in the draft on. He may therefore feel safe to state, for example, "hereinafter referred to as 'a house'". In the process of refining the draft, he may find it necessary to use the defined term somewhere in an earlier provision, bearing in mind that he has defined the term but forgetting that the definition applies only from the point in the legislation where he has introduced it. This will render the definition arguably inapplicable to cases where the word is used before the insertion point of the definition.

The expression "heretofore" must never be used. It simply means before now. In statutes it means before the legislation concerned entered into force. An expression such as "before this Act comes into force" is preferred.

2.4.5 OTHER WAYS OF PROMOTING UNDERSTANDING

2.4.5.1 DOUBLE NEGATIVES

Double negatives are cumbersome because they are a convoluted way of expressing an otherwise straightforward idea. The following examples are technically clear but take the long route:

No application may be received unless it is in Form 5.
A person other than a person referred to in section 2 is not eligible for admission to the Bar.
A person without a permit shall not take a yacht for sailing.

Unless a person is granted permission to grow a prohibited plant
he shall not do so.

The meanings of the four sentences will be more readily com-
municated if they are rewritten as follows:

An application shall be in Form 5.
Only a person referred to in section 2 is eligible for admission
to the Bar.
Only a person with a permit may take a yacht for sailing.
Only a person who has permission to grow a prohibited plant
may do so.

In the second example, one may replace "is eligible for admission" with
"may be admitted".

2.4.5.2 INDENTING AND CHAPEAUX

Some provisions start off with words which form part of the enumeration that follows them. This is sometimes referred to as a chapeau
(plural "chapeaux"). Chapeaux are of two types. For convenience, we may
classify these as opening chapeaux and terminal chapeaux. An opening
chapeau does not present much of a problem. It is normally clear that
it is only the beginning of a provision. The terminal chapeau, however,
presents certain minor inconveniences which could become large, depending on circumstances.

The following exemplifies both an opening and terminal chapeau:

A person who

(a) has been convicted of an offence involving dishonesty,

(b) has not attained the age of 21,

shall not be granted a trade licence.

This clearly means that the material appearing in the line after paragraph (b) applies both to that paragraph and paragraph (a). First, it is clear because that line goes full out to the left. Second, and obviously, it has to be so because unless the provision is so read, paragraph (a) will be left hanging. Thus even if there were a printing mistake and the phrase "shall not be granted a trade licence" were to be tagged on to (b) as a continuation of that paragraph, it would be understood to be a printing error, as the whole provision would make sense only if the phrase were read as applying to (a) as well.[30]

There will be a problem, however, if the formulation is rephrased thus:

A person shall not be granted a trade licence who

(a) has been convicted of an offence involving dishonesty,

(b) has not attained the age of 21,

except with the permission of the Minister.

Drafted this way, the terminal chapeau again applies to both. The difference is that if the chapeau were mistakenly added to (b), paragraph (a) would not be left hanging and a real interpretational problem might arise if it were alleged that there was a printing error. Grammatically, either reading will be in order. The protagonists will then either go to the office copies from which the printing was done or argue on the basis of what the context suggests, or both. In jurisdictions where a semicolon is used after each item enumerated, including the last one, the presence of a semicolon at the end of the last item suggests that the passage in question was intended to apply to both. Because of these possible problems, it is advisable to avoid the terminal chapeau whenever possible.

There is at least one other reason not to use a terminal chapeau. Especially in a long enumeration, the reader has to wait too long before the meaning of the provisions is fully revealed. Even if he realizes early that the provision has a terminal chapeau and skips ahead to it and then returns to read the rest of the enumeration, the drafter will have been inconsiderate of the reader's convenience. Most such provisions can be restructured so that the chapeau comes before the enumeration rather than after.

Punctuation is considered in a little more detail in item 2.4.5.3, but to conclude this item, the punctuating of chapeaux needs to be considered. It presents somewhat specific concerns, many of which do not fall within the area of traditional grammar.

In many jurisdictions the opening chapeau is still punctuated by a dash. For example:

Any person –

(a) who drives a motor vehicle carelessly; or

(b) who, not being a holder of a driver's licence, drives a motor vehicle;

commits an offence.

In the example, the whole provision constitutes a running sentence. According to this practice, a dash is used just before the enumeration begins. A semicolon is used at the end of each paragraph. In some jurisdictions, the end of paragraph (b) would have a comma and not a semicolon while (a) would retain its semicolon. In others, both semicolons would be replaced by commas if the sentence continues after the enumeration.

Some jurisdictions distinguish between a running sentence and a provision that consists of an introductory clause followed by an enumeration, such as:

A person wishing to appeal shall file the following:

(a) a copy of the complaint;

(b) copies of the documents he relies on.

In those jurisdictions, a colon is used in such a formulation because a list follows the introductory clause. Interestingly, in some practices, a dash is used in either case, whereas logic would dictate that the punctuation of the two formulations should be different.

The more modern practice is not to use any punctuation at the end of an opening chapeau unless it would require punctuation even without the chapeau. Thus in the second example the colon could still be used.

It is recommended that no punctuation be used as a matter of course at the end of an opening chapeau for various reasons. One is that it presents one more thing which needs to be checked in the final proofreading of draft legislation. Second, where punctuation would have been necessary or where particular punctuation would have been preferred by the drafter regardless of whether a chapeau were used, the end of the chapeau can become over-punctuated, as in

Except as provided in subsection (4), –

(a) no commercial enterprise is allowed to open on Sunday; or

(b) on a Saturday that falls on a public holiday.

A number of jurisdictions used to use both a dash and a colon (: –) to introduce an enumeration. This practice has been condemned by many authors as superfluous (in that only one of the two may be necessary) or even as extra-superfluous (in that no punctuation at all is necessary).

2.4.5.3 PUNCTUATION

Punctuation is important to any piece of writing, and legislation is no exception. In dealing with legislation, the official must be familiar with the usual rules and conventions of punctuation, as well those obtaining in the jurisdiction in which he works. If he needs to refresh his knowledge on the general aspects, he can consult a standard style and usage book, but a work written for people in the field will be more useful. In this regard, a leading work that also summarizes the relevant aspects of more bulky works is Sir Ernest Gowers's The Complete Plain Words.[31] It deals with the whole range of issues relevant to writing in official circles, including punctuation. I will deal with punctuation here, however, not only because the chapter would be incomplete without it but also because there are a few points that are particularly relevant to legislation. If the official has a sound knowledge of punctuation and is also familiar with the punctuation practices in his jurisdiction, he will be of greater assistance to the drafter in proofreading draft laws. Also, punctuation is taken into account in the interpretation of legislation though in most court cases it is referred to only to confirm a meaning that is supported by the words and syntax.[32]

(a) Full stop

The full stop – sometimes referred to as a period, even in jurisdictions that use British English – marks the end of any sentence. In legislation, it also marks the end of a section or subsection. Paragraphs and subparagraphs do not end with a full stop unless their end coincides with the end of the sentence. Beyond that, practices differ. There is an increasing tendency to omit the full stop in abbreviations. It is frequently not used in familiar initialisms such as UNDP, UNICEF and CNN, and, although some computer grammar checkers still recommend one after contractions such as Dr, St or Mrs, many publishers prefer to leave it off in those abbreviations also.

Generally speaking, apart from using it properly in certain abbreviations, such as e.g., i.e. and et al., it is not advisable to use the full stop for anything other than punctuating a sentence. For example, the full stop after "President" is unnecessary here.

I assent.

President.

A full stop is unnecessary in the arrangement of sections, as it is after a marginal note. It used to be that a full stop after a marginal note was a helpful guide when the note had become scrambled with the main provision. Apart from the fact that this now happens very rarely – because computer software enables the marginal note to be placed in a different field, and because the note is often placed above rather than to the side of the provision – even where it might occur, the value of having a full stop is not worth the inconvenience of using it.

In jurisdictions such as the United Kingdom, where the marginal note (for lack of a better term) is placed at the top in bold letters, a full stop is not used. Whatever one decides to do, it is awkward to have a full stop after marginal notes but not after each entry in the arrangement of sections, or vice versa.

A full stop should not be used in the middle of a section or subsection. If a section or subsection seems to require one, the provision is probably too long. The problem may be dealt with by placing the sentences in different provisions, unless they can be economically fused. Depending on the content, the two elements may be kept in one provision and indented.

(b) Parentheses and comma

Parentheses is a general term covering the dash, brackets and, in some uses, the comma. These marks are used to separate from the main text a section that intervenes in the main thread or interjects an aside. If the intervening part is a significant departure from the main train of thought, dashes are used at both ends. For example:

Mr Maketrouble – not that I really care about his unholy escapades – has done himself another disservice.

The grammatical dash used above is not generally used in the same way in legislation. In some jurisdictions it is not used at all as punctuation.

If the intervening passage does not depart far from the main thread, as where there is explanatory material, brackets can be used. In legislation, they are sometimes used as follows:

Where the Authority, on the grounds referred to in section 9 (relating to concealment of a material fact at the time of applying), is considering revoking a licence, it shall give the licensee 2 weeks in which to show cause why the licence should not be revoked.

This usage is for inserting explanatory matter. Brackets can also be used to modify or to achieve clarity. Here is an example from the Trade Union and Labour Relations (Consolidation) Act 1992 [UK]:

229.– ...

(4) The following statement must (without being qualified or commented upon by anything else on the voting paper) appear on every voting paper –

"If you take part in a strike or other industrial action, you may be in breach of your contract of employment."

The words in brackets are not just for convenience of reference as in the first example, where they are merely stating the subject matter of section 9. In the second example, they make it clear that even if you insert the specified words, you will still contravene the section if you add any other words relating to the subject, regardless of whether they are qualifying what is stated or just commenting upon it. Commas can also work here, but the brackets make it evident that what is between them does not constitute part of the core provision.

A fairly common use of brackets is to contain a definition:

A police officer or surveillance officer from the Department of
Corrections (in this section called "an authorised officer") may . . .

With regard to the comma, Driedger elaborated in detail the distinction between a defining clause and a non-defining clause in what
he called "strict writing". A defining (or restrictive) clause is one which
qualifies the subject; therefore no comma is placed before it. A clause
separated from the subject by commas contains what might be called ex-
traneous information and thus is non-defining (or non-restrictive). For
example, the sentence

Zambians, who are great footballers, do well on the international soccer scene

says that all Zambians are great football players and hence do well internationally. Removing the parenthetical clause leaves you with the es-
sence, "Zambians do well on the international soccer scene." If you re-
move the commas, on the other hand, the sentence says what the writer's
intention undoubtedly would have been: that those Zambians who are
great football players do well internationally.

Consider also:

The soldiers waved at the civilians who shot at them.

This sentence suggests that there were two or more groups of civilians
and that the soldiers waved at the group who shot at them. That is because, without a comma after "civilians", the phrase "who shot at them" is
qualifying, or defining, which particular group shot at the soldiers.

When a comma is placed after the word "civilians", the meaning of
the sentence changes:

The soldiers waved at the civilians, who shot at them.

That suggests that there was only one group of civilians; the soldiers waved at the group, and that group shot at the soldiers.

The following is an example from a flight attendant:

If you are interested in your front pocket there is a leaflet on safety.

Orally, there is no problem if the speaker pauses after "interested". In writing, a comma after the word would have made it clear that what was being referred to was not interest in the pocket but in safety information. While the sentence would probably not impede comprehension for long, even for people travelling by air for the first time, the reader might stop for a moment to wonder why one would be interested in his front pocket. For that reason alone, the construction is bad. All that needs to be said is that there is a safety leaflet in the seat pocket. Strictly speaking, the conditionality of the interest does not need to be mentioned.

(c) Colon and dash

In legislation the colon is used mostly to introduce a list. For example:

An applicant shall, in addition to his personal details, provide the Authority with the following:

(a) a five-year business plan;

(b) a statement outlining his experience in relation to the business for which he applies; and

(c) whether he intends to branch out into other areas of business.

Other aspects of the colon and dash have been addressed in item 2.4.5.2.

(d) Semicolon

The semicolon is a mark placed between two clauses that could otherwise be two different sentences; the semicolon's purpose is to indicate clearly the relationship between the two. In legislation it is commonly used after paragraphs and subparagraphs. The use of the semicolon in the middle of a sentence must be carefully considered. The following is an example of good use:

> The Chairperson shall take an oath before the President; the Vice-Chairperson shall take his before the Secretary to the Cabinet.

(e) Apostrophe

The following show proper use of the apostrophe:

the Managing Director's duties

the Directors' duties (where there is more than one Director)

three days' notice

(f) Hyphen

Common problems associated with use or non-use of the hyphen are covered in item 2.5.

2.5 GENERAL LINGUISTIC AND OTHER POINTS

It is worth considering a few general matters to do with language. Often the misuse or absence of punctuation can have unintentionally funny results. What exactly does this mean: "Hot Tub Sale"? Is it a sale of hot tubs, a sale of stolen tubs of some other kind, or a hotly contested sale of tubs? We can make the correct assumption because the context makes it fairly clear what is meant. Then there is the New Law Journal. Is it a law journal that is new or a journal in which the writers discuss new law?

How about the Modern Law Review? What does "End of Summer Sale" mean? Does such a sign indicate that a summer sale has been going on and that it is about to end, or is it saying "End-of-Summer Sale", meaning a sale (probably to go on for days) to mark the end of summer?

Some countries have a Serious Fraud Office. If you read this as "Serious-Fraud Office" it means the office that deals with serious frauds. If, however, one reads it as "Serious Fraud-Office" it means (however unlikely) a fraudulent office that is serious about what it does. This is nonsensical, of course, because all public offices are supposed to be serious! Linguistically, however, there are contexts in which serious ambiguity may result from such careless wording.

The sentence below has an apparent contradiction, at least in terms of function:

> The Committee shall comprise X, Y, Z and the Head of the Division in the Attorney General's Chambers responsible for commercial crime.

It appears that the division in question – and it must truly be in question – has been committing what it should be discouraging or helping to punish: commercial crime.

Is the following sentence free from ambiguity?

> Father Kariba said, two weeks before his short-lived marriage, Bishop Moza talked to him and another priest about the creation of an alternative church where priests would be given the option of marrying, a claim Moza denied yesterday.

Is it clear from this passage who had a short-lived marriage? In other words, to whom does the first possessive "his" refer?

The expression "the responsible minister" is always better written as "the minister responsible". The former may be taken to mean that some ministers are not responsible in the sense that they are not careful and serious about what they do. The same could be said of the "responsible licence holder". In these contexts, of course, no real problem arises from the double meaning, but in others the ambiguity can be problematic. The possible comic effect should be reason enough to pay careful attention to the way things are worded.

Newspapers are notorious for small slip-ups. The following comes from an actual newspaper headline: "Police Shoot Dead Man". The intended meaning was "Police Shoot Dead a Man". Whereas one will normally understand such a headline sensibly, it remains an example of poor construction and may cause far-ranging amusement. (Indeed, the unlikely meaning is not outside the realm of possibility.) There is, by contrast, no problem with "Police Shoot Dead London's Best-Known Criminal".

A common error is the misplaced modifier:

Ms Mary Mighty and Mr Michael Mite were both honoured for their achievements at the ball.

Were their achievements at the ball? No, of course not, but to ensure clarity the modifying phrase should be placed closer to the verb: "... were honoured at the ball for their achievements".

Here is an example from soccer:

He missed a second penalty.

This could mean that the same player took two penalties. He may have scored the first but missed the second or he may have missed both. It is also possible that some other player took the first penalty, which that player may or may not have scored, and the player being referred to missed the second – that is, the second which had been awarded to his team, the first having been taken by another player. To put it another way, it could mean that two penalties were awarded, one being scored and the second being missed or that two were awarded and both were missed.

It is common nowadays for the expression "Any person may" to be replaced by "A person may". The latter is said to be simpler. One should not make too much of it, but the former emphasizes equality before the law. The latter is not necessarily objectionable if one can ignore the feeling that it seems to show a desire to distinguish between humans and other beings. In the following sentence, however, the implied distinction cannot be ignored:

The Minister shall appoint a person to be Registrar.

Of course he could not appoint a being other than a member of species Homo sapiens, but it is easy to obviate the unintentional comic effect:

The Minister shall appoint a Registrar.

Moving in a rather different direction, Latin is being phased out in legal circles, though the job is by no means done. Many drafters agree that, while Latin words that have been incorporated into the English language are certainly not objectionable, if an English equivalent that is as accurate as the Latin expression is available, it should be preferred. There is, however, a danger in replacing all Latin expressions with what are simply equivalent words in English. Whereas at a literal level one may be right, at the level of communication in that particular context, it may be a failure.

An example is the use of *mutatis mutandis*. In a nutshell, this means "with necessary modifications". This substitute is sometimes used in the following way. A statute provides that the chairperson of a board is bound to disclose his interest in any matter that comes up for discussion by the board. It goes on to prescribe the procedure for doing so. A later provision seeks to apply this provision (which we shall call section 9) to the secretary of the board. To do this, the provision says, "Section 9 applies *mutatis mutandis* to the secretary." To make it "simpler" the Latin is replaced by the words "with necessary modifications". It would have been clearer, and far easier for the average person to understand, if it had stated "Section 9 applies to the secretary in the same way it applies to the chairman." Although it is not a direct translation, that is a more accurate and useful rendering of the intent of the Latin.

In certain cases, the application of a provision to a different person or circumstances without stating exactly how it will apply may introduce ambiguity. It is better to either specify the modifications that are to be made or craft a new provision specifically applying (in the example) to the secretary, even if it is repetitious in some respects.

2.5.1 VERB TENSE

Notwithstanding the use of the future tense in a lot of statutes, it is generally accepted among modern drafters that laws must be drafted in the present tense. There are at least two reasons for this. First, the present tense is much easier to deal with from the vantage point of drafting. Second, the present tense promotes ready comprehension and avoids ambiguity.

Another reason that the future tense is discouraged is that it has sometimes been understood to denote the future rather than obligation. This problem has been largely obviated by the fact that Interpretation Acts generally have a provision like that in the Interpretation Act, [NZ], whose substance is common but its brevity less so:[33]

An enactment applies to circumstances as they arise.

Thus it is both unnecessary and inadvisable to use the future tense to denote obligation.

2.5.2 "The provisions of"

Legislation commonly refers to "the provisions of this Act", "the provisions of any other law", or "the provisions of subsection (1)". The words "the provisions of" are redundant. Also, the provisions of a section are not in the same relationship to the number identifying the section as a quantity of sugar is to the bowl in which it is contained. When sugar is poured out of a bowl, the bowl continues to be an entity on its own. That is not the case with a section or other portion of a law. When the provisions of a section have been deleted, the section is no more. Accordingly, the section, subsection or other division being referred to can be cited directly without employing the words "provisions of". The position still holds where reference is to only one provision of, for example, the whole section. If there are ten ways to commit an offence under a section, it is, all other things being equal, not necessary to say "any person who contravenes any provision of this Act". It will work fine to say "any person who contravenes section 9". It will be understood that if you have contravened only one portion of that section, you have contravened that section and the Act in which it appears. It brings to mind James 2:10, where it is said that a person who breaks only one law is as a guilty as a person who has broken all the laws.

2.5.3 Statutory bodies

One is often asked what a statutory body is. The limited answer is that a statutory body is an entity created by statute. It is most commonly created by or under an Act of Parliament but may also be created by statutory instrument. In order to understand the expression fully, it is necessary to explain the legal status of a government department, a corporate statutory body and a non-corporate statutory body.

Under most Commonwealth constitutions, the chief executive is empowered to create government departments. Once created, departments constitute what may be called mainstream government. The departments generally fall under a ministry. The ministry, of course, has a minister and an administrative head generally called a Permanent Secretary. Each department has a head of department who is in charge of day-to-day administration. If one wishes to sue a department, he has to sue the government as a whole. This is because, in many jurisdictions, the government, as a legal entity, is one and indivisible. In this respect, a government can be likened to a company. A company may have a marketing department, engineering department, legal department and other departments but is still one company. If a driver in the engineering department negligently causes injury to a member of the public, the injured person must sue the company and not the engineering department. In government, too, whereas departments may in many respects function separately from one another, in the eyes of the law, they are something like the departments of one company. Although some governments have departments that are corporate bodies, for purposes of this discussion, when we refer to a department we mean one that is not constituted as a corporate body.

Then there are corporate statutory bodies. A corporate statutory body has a legal personality separate and distinct from the government. Most have a chief executive officer, who may be titled director, executive director, commissioner, commissioner general or simply chief executive – the possible titles are legion. Then there will be a policy-making body which may be called a governing body, council, commission or any other name connoting a body. The institution as a whole may be called an authority, board, council or commission. In some cases the name of the institution and the name of the policy-making organ are different. Thus the Zambia Revenue Authority has a policy-making body called the governing board.

Corporate bodies can be created either by a specific law or a general law constituting a class of bodies as corporate bodies. Where there is a specific law, it may stipulate: "There is hereby created a corporate body to be known as the Drafters Commission." A more general provision might be: "Whenever the Chief Executive creates a department under the Constitution, that department shall be a corporate body."

Finally, there are statutory bodies that are unincorporated. These are also commonly created by statute but do not have a legal personality separate from the government. For example, a minister responsible for finance may be empowered under an Income Tax Act to create a tax advisory committee to advise him on tax policy. Alternatively, the Act may state that "there is hereby established a Tax Advisory Committee". Usually the Act will give the minister guidance regarding who the members shall be (by job title or background), how many members there must be and so on. Generally, if the statute does not state that the entity is a corporate body, it is not – statutes do not normally state that the body is unincorporated. If any such body were to be sued for a wrong associated with its functions, the lawsuit would have to be against the government.

In civil service parlance, when one refers to a statutory body, the reference generally is to a corporate body rather than a non-corporate statutory body. Sometimes "independent statutory body" or a similar expression is used. The general intention behind the creation of such a body is that it should enjoy a degree of autonomy in its operations greater than that of a department or a non-corporate body.

However, the extent to which a corporate body is actually independent or autonomous will depend on the substantive provisions contained in the statute. One key area has to do with who appoints the members and to what extent their discretion is fettered. It is common to have a mixed approach. Some members may be appointed by a minister or even the President, while others may be ex-officio, that is, are members by virtue of office. For example, one of the members of a medical council may be "the Chief Medical Officer", meaning that whoever holds that post at any particular time is automatically a member. Another area that influences the degree of independence has to do with removal of office holders including, and especially, the removal or disciplining of the chief executive.

Independence is also affected by the specific provisions relating to policy and day-to-day operations. It is a fair generalization that a minister is responsible for giving the body policy directives within the general directives given by the Cabinet and within the parameters allowed by the legislation concerned. The so-called policy-making organ of the corporate body is actually responsible for interpreting and applying the policy; generally, it also oversees the running of the institution while the day-to-day administration falls under the chief executive. There are, however, some exceptions. Some statutes provide that the minister may give general or specific directions and that, if given, they shall be complied with. On the whole, therefore, the actual degree of autonomy depends on the specific provisions of the statute concerned.

Each of the entities described above will have statutory powers. A department or, more usually, the head of the department, will be invested with powers under one or more statutes. There is often an express or implied power to delegate to officers within the department or, more rarely, to persons or entities outside the government. Needless to say, statutory bodies, incorporated or unincorporated, will have powers under a statute.

In a modern government, a lot of statutory bodies are created. With respect to corporate bodies so created, it is convenient to make certain standard provisions in the law so that each statute creating a corporate body does not have to repeat the empowering provisions that every such body should have. In this regard, the Interpretation Act, Chapter 1-21, [Can], with a pinch of bilingual spice, states:

Corporations

21. (1) Words establishing a corporation shall be construed

(a) as vesting in the corporation power to sue and be sued, to contract and be contracted with by its corporate name, to have a common seal and to alter or change it at pleasure, to have perpetual succession, to acquire and hold personal property for the purposes for which the corporation is established and to alienate that property at pleasure.

(b) in the case of a corporation having a name consisting of an English and a French form or a combined English and French form, as vesting in the corporation power to use either the English or the French form of its name or both forms and to show on its seal both the English and French forms of its name or have two seals, one showing the English and the other showing the French form of its name;

(c) as vesting in a majority of the members of the corporation the power to bind the others by their acts;

and

(d) as exempting from personal liability for its debts, obligations or acts individual members of the corporation who do not contravene the provisions of the enactment establishing the corporation.

(2) Where an enactment establishes a corporation and in each of the English and French versions of the enactment the name of the corporation is in the form only of the language of that version, the name of the corporation shall consist of the form of its name in each of the versions of the enactment.

(3) No corporation is deemed to be authorized to carry on the business of banking unless that power is expressly conferred on it by the enactment establishing the corporation.

R. S., c. 1-23, s. 20

2.5.4 CRIME PROVISIONS

The drafting of penal provisions is a wide area. For our present purposes, only a few more commonly encountered matters need to be noted. One is that usually an Interpretation Act will provide that wherever a penalty is provided, that penalty is the maximum penalty. For example, a provision might say:

A person who steals commits an offence and is liable to imprisonment for two years.

This does not mean that a two-year sentence will be imposed for every offence but that two years' incarceration is the maximum penalty. The same applies to a fine. The provision in the Interpretation Act obviates the necessity of always stating that the sentence is only a maximum. Also, Interpretation Acts sometimes provide that when a fine and a custodial sentence are prescribed for the same offence, a court may impose both. Needless to say, there will also be a guide issued by some authority regarding the principles of sentencing, or case law enunciating the principles of sentencing. In certain jurisdictions, for example, case law suggests that where there is an option of a fine, a court should, for a first offender, normally impose a fine unless there are aggravating circumstances.

Often it is not convenient to state a penalty in each provision. The drafter may specify a penalty in selected cases, while in other cases stating merely that a particular act is an offence. If he does the latter, the official has to look for a provision whose marginal note will be something like "General penalty" and which may read:

Where a person is convicted of an offence under this Act for which no specific penalty is provided, he is liable to a fine of three hundred dollars or one month's imprisonment.

Such a provision will sometimes be found in the Part of the Act entitled "Miscellaneous".

The official needs also to notice the difference between a provision such as the one cited above and one which states:

> A person who contravenes a provision of this Act commits an offence.

This latter provision criminalizes any contravention, while the former applies only if there is a separate provision which specifically states that the doing of a particular act is an offence. Under the latter provision, the minister commits an offence if he does not comply with a provision such as:

> The Minister shall, within one month of receiving the application, convey his decision to an applicant.

Use of the latter provision, therefore, calls for caution.

2.5.5 Definition of terms

In written laws, definitions are common. They are used to give technical meanings to terms, to clear up in advance possible ambiguities that may arise from the use of certain terms and to avoid repetition. To use the simplest of examples, one may be drafting legislation which will apply to turtles. To make it clear, he may define that expression as including turtle eggs. When he does so, it will not only clarify a possible ambiguity but will also make it unnecessary to always refer to "turtles and eggs of turtles".

Perhaps the most basic feature of definitions is whether they use the word "means" or "includes". Generally speaking, a definition that uses the former suggests that it is exhaustive while the latter admits of other things that are not itemized but are generally understood to be included in the expression.[34] It is now well established that a definition that says a term "means and includes" is on this logic contradictory. However, a judicious use of each term in different places of the same definition is acceptable.

The case of *Board of Inland Revenue v Young (Selwyn)* [35] exemplifies some of the issues relating to the two words. Section 2(1) of the Income Tax Act provided, among other things, that:

> "management charges" means charges made for the provision of management services and includes charges made for the provision of personal services and technical and managerial skills.

The question arose as to whether the words "and includes" had the effect of extending the definition of management charges to charges that were not for the provision of management services, but were for the provision either of personal services or technical or managerial services.

Chief Justice de la Bastide (as he then was) saw it in this way:

> It is well known that the word 'includes' or 'including' in a definition may be used to achieve a variety of different results. In what may be described as the classic and most orthodox use of that term, the purpose it serves is to pre-empt any ambiguity that may arise as to whether something falls within or without the definition preceding those words. I suppose an example of this usage might be the case (referred to in argument) of the definition of a 'street', which provided that it was to include a highway. In other cases, the word 'includes' is used really for no other purpose than to provide illustrations of things which fall within the definition and which would be considered to fall within it in any event on a normal construction of language.[36]

The judge went on to say that:

There are, however, some cases in which the use of the word 'includes' has a more drastic effect, and that is when it is used to include things which could never be considered on a normal interpretation to fall within the definition as it stands up to the point where the word 'includes' or 'including' is used; that is when it has the deeming effect. In my view, a court should only construe the word 'includes' as having that deeming effect if the definition cannot be construed sensibly in such a way as to give it any other effect. In other words, if what follows the word 'includes' can sensibly and reasonably be treated as subject to the constraints imposed by whatever defining words precede the word 'includes' or 'including', then that is the proper way of construing the definition.[37]

Finally he decided:

In this case it is perfectly possible to envisage that management services may be provided in a way which involves the provision of personal services or of technical skills and, obviously, of managerial skills. And, therefore, it is unnecessary, for the purpose of making sense of this definition, to treat what follows the words 'and includes' as applying to services which are not management services. The effect of the definition, therefore, is simply in my view to emphasize that, if personal services or technical and managerial skills are provided for purposes which would qualify as purposes connected with the management of the taxpayer company or firm, they are properly to be regarded as services the charges for which will be treated as management charges for the purposes of the Income Tax Act.[38]

These observations are sound as far as the reality of the contexts in which the two words are used and how courts often are forced into stilted interpretation in order to do justice. However, from the perspective of drafting practice in relation to use of both terms in a definition, a good drafter always tries to ensure that the words coming after "includes" help to clarify matters that may not clearly fall under the words coming after "means". In other words, he must use the second part of the definition to clarify any matters that may not clearly fall within the core part of the definition. If it is clear to the drafter that the two elements are not related, then he must either have a definition with different elements such as (a), (b) and so on, or work with two definitions. It is also worth noting that in the rare cases where "includes" can be used to introduce an exhaustive definition, the problem is likely to be one of fixing a bad drafting practice or the need to do justice in an exotic problem.

A problem for the official arises when he is not conscious of the fact that a term is defined. It is amazing how even lawyers have often advised erroneously merely because they did not look to see if the term was defined. We have stated elsewhere that many terms are defined in an Interpretation Act, and these will apply unless the particular law specifically defines the same terms differently or something in the context suggests otherwise. For this reason, even before resorting to the Interpretation Act, the official will need to check whether the Act he is dealing with itself defines the term at issue. Central to this is where to find a definition.

An Act of some size usually has a section called "Definitions" or "Interpretation", which contains all or most of the expressions used. In many jurisdictions, this is section 2 of the legislation; in others, it is found towards the end of the legislation. However that may be, the official needs to look first in the section he is examining. This is because even if a term is defined in the interpretation section, occasionally it is used in one section to mean a different thing in that section alone. Especially in large legislation, in addition to the general interpretation section there may be some definitions applying only to one Part of the legislation. These may be at the beginning or the end of the Part. If there is a definition that applies only to a section, it is common to have it in the last subsection of the relevant section. In some jurisdictions the definition or definitions are sometimes in a section immediately after the section in which the expression is used. The official needs to know all these possibilities so that he can ascertain what the practice is in his jurisdiction. Even after he establishes what the practices may be, he is well advised to check all these possibilities each time, for practices do change from time to time and sometimes (in small measure) from drafter to drafter.

Further on definitions, often a drafter will encounter the wording:

"game", in relation to gambling, means . . .

Whereas this provision suggests that the word is used in other contexts, necessitating the use of the words "in relation to gambling", it is worth noting that such definitions are sometimes used (erroneously) even where the word is not used in relation to anything else. The phrase "in relation to" is necessary only if the word is used in relation to other substantive matters. When such a double definition appears to be necessary, it is advisable to use another word or expression.

It must be remembered that when the law being examined is a statutory instrument and not an Act, the expressions in the statutory instrument have the same meaning as in the Act unless otherwise stated. This is dealt with in item 3.4.1. More detailed discussion of how to deal with definitions can be found elsewhere.[39]

2.5.6 GENDER-NEUTRAL LAWS

Interpretation Acts often provided that words importing the masculine gender included females and that the converse was also true.[40] Progress continues to be made in the Commonwealth towards equality in legislative expression. In the older Commonwealth countries, much greater progress has been made. The Interpretation Act, Chapter 1-21, [Can.], in section 33 (1), provides:

Words importing female persons include male persons and corporations and words importing female persons include male persons and corporations.

This provision shows us that males need not always be mentioned first in legislation.

A provision on the same subject in Australia is even more encompassing. Perhaps to ensure that all biological possibilities are covered, as they should be, the Acts Interpretation Act 1901, section 23 (a), states:

Words importing a gender include every other gender.

The Acts Interpretation Act, 1901, [Aus], further provides:

How Chairs and Deputy Chairs may be referred to

18B (1) Where an Act establishes an office of Chair of a body, the Chair may be referred to as Chair, Chairperson, Chairman, Chairwoman or by any other such term as the person occupying the office so chooses.

(2) If a person occupying an office mentioned in subsection (1) does not make known his or her choice of term, the person may be referred to by whichever of the following terms that a person addressing that person considers appropriate:

(a) Chair;

(b) Chairperson;

(c) Chairman;

(d) Chairwoman.

Similar provision is made for Deputy Chair. In this general regard, section 31 of the Interpretation Act 1999, [NZ], provides that:

> In an enactment passed or made before the commencement of this Act, words denoting the masculine gender include females.

Quite apart from the Interpretation Acts, many countries now have policies on gender-neutral expression in all legislation. Some have adopted policies to move towards gender neutrality while others have a strict policy that all legislation should be gender neutral. In Australia, New South Wales was the first jurisdiction to adopt gender-neutral language in legislation. In 1983 the Attorney General approved a proposal from the Parliamentary Counsel's Office that in the preparation of future legislation preference would be given to the use of gender-neutral language. That policy was announced by the Governor on 16 August 1983. Since then it has been "strictly applied in the Office".[41]

The United Kingdom Office of the Parliamentary Counsel has recommended that: "Government Bills are to take a form which achieves gender-neutral drafting so far as it is practicable, at no more than a reasonable cost to brevity or intelligibility. It is recognised that in practice a flexible approach to this change will need to be adopted (for example, in at least some of the cases where existing legislation is being amended)."[42]

2.6 STRUCTURAL CHECK

Once a draft has been completed, the final stage is to check its structure. At this stage what is needed is a final examination to ensure that it is well expressed and well written, and that everything that should have gone in has gone in. Conceptually this can be divided into four processes. Each drafter has to assess these and determine what works best for him. These processes will naturally overlap in practice; however, a systematic approach as suggested below will yield dividends.

First, it is crucial to ensure that the manner in which the legislation is to come into force and related matters such as transitional provisions are checked. A piece of legislation can be fine in every respect, but if the time and manner in which it comes into force are chaotic, all the good efforts of the drafter and his instructing officials come to naught – at least at the law's entry into force. Thus the drafter and the official need to make sure that there is a commencement provision and appropriate transitional provisions, unless the particular piece of legislation does not need them. The matter, however, should be considered in every draft that is prepared.

Second, those provisions whose checking calls for flipping must be checked next. This can be divided into three parts:

(a) Numbering and lettering of the whole law. Initially, the drafter needs to check the sequence of numbering of substantive provisions from the first provision to the last. In an Act, the numbering of sections should be checked first and corrected if necessary because much will depend on it, especially in terms of cross-references.

(b) Harmony between table of contents and labels in the draft. The arrangement of sections or regulations, as the case may be, should be checked to ensure that it agrees in terms of both numbering and the words of the labels. It must be noted that, once provisions have been drafted and marginal notes or headings put in place, some custom made or commercially available computer programmes can generate an arrangement of sections or regulations on command. Some of these are not perfect and will include everything in the margin, including material that should not appear in the arrangement, such as references to chapter numbers of the laws. Computer-generated arrangements have to be thoroughly checked, and may need to be manually adjusted.

(c) Internal numbering of each provision. Once (a) and (b) have been completed, a check of each provision is needed to ensure that the internal numbering is in order. In other words, the subsections, paragraphs and subparagraphs must be checked to make sure that they are correct in all respects, including cross-references internal to each provision.

(d) Correctness of the internal and external cross-references of the draft as a whole. These should have been checked initially as the draft was being prepared. However, it is advisable to check the cross-references as a separate exercise and, in that process, recheck the substantive effect of the particular provisions containing cross-references. It is unbelievably easy to make wrong cross-references, especially where the relationship between two or more provisions is not as straightforward as it is when referring to a regulation-making power or a power to make an appointment. In relationships that take a little figuring out, a section that is incorrect but has content similar to the one that should be cited often winds up being cited instead.

Third, the draft can now be read from the beginning to the end. In this process, there should be two distinct activities taking place. As he reads the draft, the drafter must continuously check (electronically to the extent practicable):

(a) Consistency of language. The words and expressions used in relation to the same thing must be consistent, and where something else is meant a different word or expression must be used.

(b) Use of definitions. If a term is defined it must be used as much as possible in the way it is defined. For instance, if "Director" is defined to mean "the Director of the Institute for Research", the draft must refer to the Director and not set out the full title. If a "house" is defined to include an apartment, then the expression "house" must be used throughout and there should be no reference to "house or apartment".

(c) Consistency of capitalization. Of course, all words that grammatically must be capitalized must be capitalized. In cases where capitalization is optional, a decision must be made whether to capitalize and thereafter the draft must remain consistent.

(d) Spelling. Needless to say, the computer can assist in correcting spelling. It is important to remember, however, which version of English the draft is written in. Further, autocorrect programmes are well known to automatically change certain words (including some added to the system by the drafter) but not all words. In some cases the spellchecker will correct or highlight words or expressions that do not need to be corrected, even if one is using the right English software dictionary.

(e) Accuracy of names of places, offices and other similar words. This could be done by flipping back and forth but is best checked when one is reading through, as only then is the drafter sure to notice all such expressions. The find and replace command in the relevant computer programme can be used as appropriate.

As the draft is being read and the above checks are being carried out, certain things need to be checked periodically:

(a) Suitability of headings and marginal notes. It is advisable to read the heading or marginal note first and then read the provision, thereafter going back to the heading or marginal note for one last look.

(b) Anything that catches the eye. A mere gaze on a page with a slight pause may help identify certain kinds of errors, some of which a computer will highlight.

(c) That the contents of subsections, paragraphs and sub-paragraphs are in logical sequence. Within each subparagraph, the sequence of enumerated items or items in a series must be logical.

Fourth, after all the provisions have been checked, the drafter needs to verify the following:

(a) Accuracy of the long title. Just as the legislature rechecks the long title once changes have been made to a Bill, the drafter and official must do the same.

(b) Adequacy and appropriateness of the Objects and Reasons. Because the objects have even more detail than the long title, it is almost always necessary to check them again after even minor substantive changes have been made to the Bill.

(c) Consistency of penal provisions. A thorough check specifically of penalties is necessary and must be reflected upon separately. Often the types of activities that may be captured by a particular penal provision may not be immediately apparent without meditating on them. Also, the imprisonment provisions and the fines must make sense from provision to provision. Unless there is a really good reason, if one provision says the offender is liable to six months' imprisonment or a fine of ten thousand dollars, another should not specify a penalty of one hundred thousand dollars for the same period of imprisonment.

(d) Any other specific matters. These will be matters such as such as chapeaux, to ensure that they did not get gobbled up by the main provision.[43]

On the whole, proofreading, especially of large legislation, is a painstaking business. Generally, a drafter will not let a draft go without having another drafter examine it for its total quality in terms of the implementation of the legislative scheme and for any grammatical and typographical errors. In some offices, to keep the peace, the second drafter is generally limited to proofreading. In other offices, the drafter commenting can raise any issue but must leave it with the drafter who drew the legislation to decide what to do.

It is important to take into account several things in dealing with the editorial quality of laws. First, only so much can be done within a certain period of time. It is sometimes recommended that one proofreader not read more than a certain number of pages within a certain space of time. If more than the recommended number is attempted, the number of errors that go unnoticed will increase.

Second, no matter how careful one is, the drafter's overall volume of work will affect the quality of his proofreading. Time must be made or set aside to ensure accurate proofreading of laws. This is a perennial problem in developing jurisdictions, even with computerization, because of the acute shortage of drafting staff and, in many cases, the lack of editorial staff.

Third, the official must not assume that once a law leaves the drafter's desk it is perfect. He must read it in detail as if it were his own and satisfy himself that it is, among other things, editorially in order. While the implementing of the instructions in a manner that is legally workable is the primary responsibility of the drafter, the editorial quality of the law is a joint responsibility shared equally between the drafter (and support staff) and the client ministry. Thus when Parliamentary Counsel sends it out to the client institution, he will be wise to state in his correspondence that the institution must also read it carefully to ensure that it is in order editorially and not just with respect to the substance of the proposals. Some offices have a standard form for this portion of the memorandum. Others state this in a handbook or other relevant guidelines.

Notes

1. In the UK, many years ago, Sir Ernest Gowers was tasked by the government to write a treatise that would be used by civil servants to improve the way they wrote. It resulted in the classic work that eventually became known as *The Complete Plain Words* (see note 31 below).

2. As to the making of proposals before drafting begins and reviewing of drafts, see generally Bilika H. Simamba, *The Legislative Process: A Handbook for Public Officials* (Bloomington, Indiana: AuthorHouse, 2009), Chap 2. See also Michael Zander, *The Law-Making Process*, 6ᵗʰ ed. (1980; repr. Cambridge: Cambridge University Press, 2004, 2006).

3. See more fully the reproduction of that work in E.A. Driedgar, *Legislative Forms and Precedents*, 2ⁿᵈ ed. (Ottawa, Ontario: Department of Justice, 1976), 321-378.

4. The example is of the author's own devising.

5. Thornton, *Legislative Drafting*, 4ᵗʰ ed. (London, Dublin, Edinburgh: Butterworths 1996), 22.

6. On how to amend schedules and how to give instructions, see item 5.2.5.2 and 2.3, respectively, in Simamba, n2.

7. Section 23 of the Interpretation Act 1999, [NZ]. See also Interpretation Act, Chapter 1-21, [Can], s 40 (2).

8. Section 29, Interpretation Act 1999, [NZ], which says an enactment "means the whole or a portion of an Act or regulations".

9. For convenience here we will use this term. However, it is acknowledged that some jurisdictions do not put the indications in the margin but on top of the provision.

10. This technically now stands repealed after incorporation of the amendment into the principal Act.

11. See also Interpretation Act, Cap. 2, [Zam], s 4 (3); and Acts Interpretation Act 1901, [Aus], s 23 (b).

12. *C.O. Williams Construction Ltd v Blackman and Another* (1994) WIR 94 (Privy Council case from Barbados).

13. Income Tax (Amendment) Act, No 11 of 1996, [BVI], s 2, repealing and replacing s 25 of the Income Tax Act, Cap. 206. There can be no excuse for a professional drafter making such a mistake.

14. Incidentally, there are those who consider "despite" too casual for legislation while others consider "notwithstanding" to be prudish even in legislation.

15. Thornton, *Legislative Drafting*, 102n5.

16. Ibid., 85.

17. Bees Act, R.S.O. 1990, c.B6, s. 25.

18. Charitable Institutions Act, R.S.O. 1990, c.C9, s.12.

19. Law Reform Commission of Victoria, 1987, Report 9, *Plain English and the Law*, p 61.

20. Thornton, *Legislative Drafting*, 101n5.

21. Michèle Asprey, *Plain Language for Lawyers*, 3rd ed. (Sydney: Federation Press, 2003), 196n9.

22. See example in item 3.4.2.5.

23. F. Reed Dickerson, *The Fundamentals of Legal Drafting*, 2nd ed. (Boston and Toronto: Little, Brown and Company, 1986), 101, 102, quoted in Thornton, *Legislative Drafting*, 24n5.

24. Thornton, *Legislative Drafting*, 24n5.

25. But see Interpretation Act 1999 of New Zealand, s 8(2), which says that the Act does not specify a date of entry into force the Act enters into force the day after assent; and s 9(2) which says if a regulation does not specify a date, it enters into force the day after notification in the Gazette.

26. For example words such as "over", "under" and so on.

27. See also ss 35, 36 and 37 of Acts Interpretation Act 1901, [Aus].

28. Cap. 2.

29. Thornton, *Legislative Drafting*, 92–93n5.

30. There are many court authorities that suggest that when there is an obvious error in the printing of a statute, the court will apply the statute as if the error were corrected. For example, if a cross-reference is clearly wrong, the court will apply it as if corrected. See P. St J. Langan, *Maxwell on the Interpretation of Statutes*, 12th ed. (Bombay: N.M. Tripathi Private Ltd, 1976), 230–32; see also item 3.4.2.11.

31. 3rd ed. (London: H.M. Stationery Office, 1986; Harmondsworth: Penguin Books, 1987). Citations are to the Penguin edition.

32. See *Douglas (Clayton) v The Police* (1992) 43 WIR 175 (East Carib. Ct. of App.).

33. Section 6.

34. But see *Caldow Properties Ltd v HJG Low and Associates* [1971] NZLR 311 as to how "includes" can herald an exhaustive definition.

35. (1997) 53 WIR 335.

36. Ibid., 336.

37. Ibid., 336 – 337.

38. Ibid., 337.

39. Bilika H. Simamba, "The Placing and Other Handling of Definitions", *Statute L R* 27, no. 2 (2006): 73.

40. Section 6 (a) and (b) of the Interpretation Act 1978, [UK]. Some jurisdictions retain the one-sided provision that words importing the masculine gender include females but not the other way around; an example is s 4 (2) of the Interpretation Act, Cap 2, [Zam].

41. Accessed from http://www.pco.nsw.gov.au/about.htm on 13 March, 2008. See link "plain language" for *New South Wales Parliamentary Counsel's Office, Policies relating to Plain Language and gender-neutral expression*, May 2000, 4.

42. See *Newsletter of the Commonwealth Association of Legislative Counsel*, February 2009, 43 at 48 where the policy is quoted. See also reference there to secondary legislation.

43. See item 2.4.5.2.

CHAPTER 3
INTERPRETATION OF STATUTES

3.1 INTRODUCTION

Loosely speaking, when one is reading a statute, he reads it in the first instance giving the words their ordinary meaning in the language of the statute. However, because statutes do sometimes give special meanings to certain words or expressions, he must ensure that the provision that seems to be relevant to his inquiry does not contain a word or words that the statute gives a meaning that is different from that which may first occur to him. For example, when you refer to a "house" many people will immediately think of a fixed structure, and yet a statute, depending on what it is trying to achieve, may define the term as including a mobile home. Whereas a term may not be defined in the Act, it may be defined in a separate Act commonly called an Interpretation Act. And even there the term may not be defined. At that point, if the issue remains unresolved, one has to resort to court cases.

Cases may contain not just what the term may have been held to mean in previous cases but also the approaches to resolving ambiguities. The former guide an official in applying a particular law: The later equip the official with the tools necessary to approach the interpretation of any law intelligently and using legal principles. A person drafting laws or interpreting them often has to deal more with the approaches to statutory interpretation than with the meaning of particular words in particular contexts. It is for this reason that this chapter deals with the various approaches to the reading and applying of statutes.

The whole subject of statutory interpretation is wide, complex and ever-changing. However, I have had to advise on certain rules more frequently than on others because they are more commonly encountered in drafting and applying legislation. For this reason, the discussion in this chapter will concentrate on those rules that are, in my experience, most frequently encountered in dealing with proposals for legislation or applying enacted laws.

The following are some of the issues that arise in reading statutes. If the apparent intention behind a statute is clear but the words used seem to fall short of giving full effect to that intention, to what extent can a court go to remedy the deficiency? Conversely, if the words of the statute are clear but seem to water down or defeat the intention of its makers, to what extent can the court pursue the intention in the face of the words actually used? Is a state bound by the laws it passes? Where a statute falls for interpretation before a court and its provisions are in conflict with an international agreement, what should the court do? Is the international agreement relevant? If it is, to what extent can it be given effect, if at all? The official attempting a draft or who is reading a statute must be aware of at least some of the rules so he can guide himself accordingly.

Although an Interpretation Act often elucidates the meaning of some otherwise obscure provisions, there are a lot more rules contained in cases decided by courts. At a basic level, one needs to read the Interpretation Act in his jurisdiction for it will contain the answers to some of these questions and numerous others that officials tend to ask from time to time as they deal with legislative drafters. Then the Interpretation Act has to be buttressed by some key approaches as enunciated by the courts and which may not have been reduced to statute or which, even if dealt with in the Act, will be illustrated by court cases.

3.2 SUPREMACY OF PARLIAMENT AND OF THE CONSTITUTION

3.2.1 GENERAL

In England Parliament was said to be supreme in two senses – and I say "was", for the legal order has changed somewhat. First, Parliament was the highest law-making body. There were, and still are, persons and authorities that also make law, but they exercise legislative power that is delegated to them by Parliament – hence the expression "delegated legislation". As these persons and authorities are subordinate to Parliament, an alternative term is "subordinate legislation". Delegated or subordinate legislation is not principal legislation but is subsidiary to principal legislation, and is therefore also called "subsidiary legislation". Second, Parliament was supreme in that it had power to make any law on any subject and to any effect, and no person or body outside it had the power to call that into legal question.

As is well known, Britain has no written constitution; thus supremacy of that kind was possible and perhaps unavoidable. Where there is a written constitution, Parliament does not hold the same kind of supremacy. In that case, the constitution is supreme, and the courts can call into legal question anything, including any law that is passed by Parliament, which is considered by a litigant to be unconstitutional. In other words, although Parliament is the highest law-making body, it, too, has to exercise its powers in accordance with the substantive and procedural limitations contained in the constitution. Constitutions typically provide that the constitution is the supreme law and any other law that is inconsistent with it is void to the extent of the inconsistency.[1]

Let us now consider Parliament as a legislative body in the British Commonwealth vis-à-vis the other organs of government. The classical distinction, of course, is that the legislature makes laws, the executive implements those laws and, in the case of a dispute, the courts interpret the laws. In adjudicating a dispute, the court is merely supposed to interpret the law. It should not attempt to make law, for in that area Parliament is supreme (subject to what follows regarding the legal status in the United Kingdom of certain instruments issued by the European Union). The rules and principles of statutory interpretation are said to be aimed at finding out the intention of Parliament. It is also the case that rules and principles of statutory interpretation are applicable to statutory instruments, the only variation being that a statutory instrument has to be interpreted keeping in mind the provisions of the enabling Act – that is, the Act under which the instrument is made.

The supremacy of Parliament does not mean, as we have observed, that no other person or authority may make laws. For example, Article 80 (1) of the Constitution of Zambia provides that:

(1) Nothing in Article 62 shall prevent Parliament from conferring on any person or authority power to make statutory instruments.

That is a common provision in constitutions.

In some jurisdictions the doctrine of supremacy of Parliament never existed and in others it has not survived. Certain countries, including some Scandinavian countries, allow an adjudicating authority to "fill in the gaps" to an extent that is more drastic than one may find in the British Commonwealth. The public official merely needs to find out what the position is in his jurisdiction. However, generally speaking, in the British Commonwealth the concept of parliamentary supremacy remains intact, and the whole matter of statutory interpretation is said to be about ensuring that parliamentary intention is carried out. The extent to which this principle has been affected in the United Kingdom is dealt with in item 3.4.2.2.

3.2.2 INTENTION OF PARLIAMENT

Since the concept of parliamentary supremacy dictates that parliamentary intent be ascertained and effected, the official or the drafter must determine where and how this intention is to be found. In the words of E.A. Driedger:

> The "intention of Parliament" is, in a sense, a fiction. It has not an intention formulated by the mind of Parliament, for Parliament has no mind; and it is not the collective intention of the Members of Parliament for no such collective intention exists. The only real intention is the intention of the sponsors of the Bill that gave rise to the Act: but that is not the intention of Parliament. The "intention of Parliament" can only be an agreement by the majority that the words in the Bill express what is known as the intention of Parliament.[2]

In the same vein, in *DPP v. Schildcamp*,[3] Lord Reid said that an Act as a whole must be seen as a product of "the whole legislative process" and, viewed in this light, "we are searching for the intention of the draftsman rather than the intention of Parliament".

Further, a law can be applied to a state of affairs that did not exist at the time it was passed. For example, a scientific invention that did not exist at the time of the passing of an Act may be held to be within the scope of that Act. This emphasizes the partly fictional nature of what we call the intention of Parliament. In this regard, the words of Lord Wilberforce in *Royal College of Nursing v. Department of Health* are instructive:

In interpreting an Act of Parliament it is proper, and indeed necessary, to have regard to the state of affairs existing, and known by Parliament to be existing, at the time. It is a fair presumption that Parliament's policy or intention is directed to that state of affairs. Leaving aside cases of omission by inadvertence, this being not such a case when a new state of affairs, or a fresh set of facts bearing on policy, come into existence, the courts have to consider whether they fall within the parliamentary intention. They may be held to do so if they fall within the same genus of facts as to those which the expressed policy has been formulated. They may also be held to do so if there can be detected a clear purpose in the legislation which can only be fulfilled if the extension is made. How liberally these principles may be applied must depend on the nature of the enactment, and the strictness or otherwise of the words in which it has been expressed. The court should be less willing to extend express meanings if it is clear that the Act in question was designed to be restrictive or circumscribed in its operation rather than liberal or permissive. They will be much less willing to do so where the new subject-matter is different in kind or dimension from that for which the legislation was passed. In any event there is one course which the courts cannot take under the law of this country; they cannot fill gaps; they cannot by asking the question, "what would Parliament have done in this current case, not being one in contemplation, if the facts had been before it?", attempt themselves to supply the answer, if the answer is not to be found in the terms of the Act itself.[4]

Parliamentary intention is an enigmatic thing. Where it is clear, we seem never to speak of it. When it is unclear, we cannot but speak of it. In practice there seem to be at least three kinds of parliamentary intent. The first we may call patent intention. This is a case where the intention is clear, no interpretational problem arises, and therefore there may be little or no discussion in the context of statutory interpretation. The second we may call fictional intention. This is where members of the legislature did not agree at all on an issue or did not specifically debate it, but we surmise their intention, knowing that they are intelligent and purposeful people. And finally, we have semi-fictional intention, where, for example, they agreed on the ends to be met but not the means of achieving them. In this latter case, the arguments would be about which means they would have had in mind.

3.3 RULES OF STATUTORY INTERPRETATION

The rules that the courts have developed guide them in ascertaining the intention of Parliament. In fact, some of the rules that appear in Interpretation Acts were developed by the courts. However, as stated above, there are numerous rules of interpretation that are not enacted. The rules (both enacted and in case law) are essential to the understanding of statutes. The three classical rules will now be considered in turn.[5]

3.3.1 THE MISCHIEF RULE

The mischief rule was famously expounded in *Heydon's Case*.[6] Under this rule, the courts search for the remedy laid down by Parliament for a shortcoming in the common law and the rationale for the remedy. In the words of Coke, "cases out of the letter of the statute, yet within the same mischief, or cause of the making of the same, shall be within the same remedy that the statute provideth".[7] This approach, sometimes called "equitable construction", predominated in the fifteenth and sixteenth centuries. The application of the rule in some cases was criticized because courts paid too much attention to what they rightly or wrongly perceived as the intention of Parliament and then proceeded to do violence to the statute by giving it a meaning that was far-fetched. In Driedger's words, "the judges paid more attention to the 'spirit' than to the letter. Having found the mischief they proceeded to make mischief with the words of the statute."[8]

3.3.2 THE LITERAL RULE

Then, as Miers and Page have pointed out, there was a shift towards arguments based on the actual words used. They state, "This shift began following the emergence of the doctrine of legislative supremacy of Parliament and was considerably hastened by more exact drafting styles in the nineteenth century."[9]

The literal rule received perhaps its most famous enunciation in the *Sussex Peerage Case*.[10] Basically, this rule states that where a statute is clear and unambiguous, all that is necessary is to apply it in accordance with the natural and ordinary meaning of the words used. The court, it is said, must not try to change or strain the meaning of these words in an attempt to give them an effect that the court thinks they should have. However, if the meaning of the words is not clear, the court may try to find the meaning that best accords with what is perceived as the intention of Parliament but which the words are still capable of bearing. The literal rule was often criticized on the basis that in applying it courts often became rigid and did not pay much attention to the real intention of Parliament. It has also been criticized on the reasoning that words cannot always be clear and unambiguous until they are read in their entire context.

3.3.3. THE GOLDEN RULE

Then there is the golden rule, which is that a statute, or in fact any legal document, must be read harmoniously – that is, in such a way as to ensure that one part of it does not conflict with another. To do this, a court will sometimes narrow or expand the meaning of a term if that will ensure that the whole law will have harmony within itself. In the words of Lord Wensleydale in *Grey v. Pearson,*

> In construing wills and indeed statutes, and all written instruments, the grammatical and ordinary sense of the words is to be adhered to, unless that would lead to some absurdity, or some repugnance or inconsistency with the rest of the instrument, in which case the grammatical and ordinary sense of the words may be modified, so as to avoid the absurdity and inconsistency, but no farther.[11]

The operation of this rule may need illustration. Imagine that a law states: "It is the function of the Fisheries Commission to regulate *marine resources.*" Another section states that the Chief Conservation and Fisheries Officer of the commission "is responsible for the conservation and regulation of *fish*". Obviously, "marine resources" is much wider than "fish" and could include non-living resources. Faced with such an apparent discrepancy, a court has to either widen the meaning of "fish" to include other living marine resources, or narrow the meaning of "marine resources" in this particular case by holding it to refer only to fish. In the context of a Fisheries Act, the court may well decide that "marine resources" must be narrowed down to fish only. Such an approach will be necessary to avoid the absurdity that the scope of the functions of the Fisheries Commission – in effect the scope of the Act – would be different from the duties of its chief executive officer.

3.3.4 THE LATEST APPROACH

The rules outlined above, while they have not been abandoned, have now been somewhat rationalized. In the words of Lord Simon in *Ealing London Borough Council v. Race Relations Board,*

The courts have principal avenues of approach to the ascertainment of the legislative intention: (1) examination of the social background, as specifically proved if not within the common knowledge, in order to identify the social or juristic defect which is the likely subject of the remedy; (2) a conspectus of the entire relevant body of the law for the same purpose; (3) particular regard to the long title of the statute to be interpreted (and, where available, the preamble), in which the general legislative objects will be stated; (4) scrutiny of the actual words to be interpreted in the light of the established canons of interpretation; (5) examination of the other provisions of the statute in question (or other statutes in *pari materia*) for the light which they throw on the particular words which are the subject of interpretation.[12]

One of Driedger's formulations helps to state the new rule (simplified here) using terminology we have used above. He says that the modern principle of the interpretation of statutes, as he called it, is that an Act as a whole is to be read in its entire context so as to ascertain the intention of Parliament (literal rule), the object of the Act (the mischief rule) and the scheme of the Act (the golden rule). In other words, the three classical rules are combined and given equal emphasis. Generally speaking, this is the latest approach to the interpretation of statutes.

In the same connection, the words of Lord Griffith in *Pepper v. Hart* must also be noticed:

The days are long passed when the courts adopted a strict constructionist view of interpretation which required them to adopt the literal meaning of the language. The courts must adopt a purposive approach which seeks to give effect to the true purpose of legislation.[13]

This latest approach is more commonly referred to as the purposive approach and is gaining ground in different parts of the British Commonwealth. In the Australian case of *Black v Black* [14] the spouses entered into a financial arrangement before marriage. The arrangement had to comply with the Family Law Act 1975 [Aust]. Upon the parties becoming enstranged, the wife sought to enforce certain provisions of the agreement. Section 90G(1)(b) of the Act provided as one of the requirements that:

> b. The agreement contains, in relation to each party to the agreement, a statement to the effect that the party to whom the agreement relates has been provided, before the agreement was signed by him or her, as certified in an annexure to the agreement, with independent legal advice from the legal practitioner as to [certain matters]. . .

These matters included, inter alia, that it was prudent to enter into the agreement and that its provisions were fair and prudent.

The necessary certificate from the husband's solicitor was provided prior to the husband initially signing the agreement on 2 September 2002. However, on 3 September 2002 the wife saw her solicitor and raised an objection in relation to clause 17 which initially read:

> 17. During the period of cohabitation [the wife] and [husband] wished to share in equal proportions all electricity, gas, telephone and other household outgoings and all food and household supplies for their joint living but will otherwise separately maintain themselves and their children. [15]

The clause beginning with "but will otherwise. . ." was removed and the wife signed and dated it. This was in effect a rejection by the wife of the counter offer made by the husband. Following that change, the husband's solicitor did not prepare a new certificate under section 90G(1)(b).

The husband argued, among other things, that: (a) upon the agreement being prepared without the objectionable clause, a new certificate should have been prepared by the husband's then solicitor; (b) the agreement must be strictly construed, that is, since there was no new certificate issued after the amendment was effected, the agreement was void. This last argument, it was said, was on the basis that such agreements are unique in that, if binding, they excluded courts from exercising certain powers under Part VIII of the Act to make adjustive orders.

The court considered the purposive approach to the interpretation of statutes. It noted the history of the approaches in Australia as set out by DS Pearce and RS Geddes,[16] which can be paraphrased as follows: (a) The purposive approach was applied by determining the purpose of the Act, or the particular provision in question (the "mischief" with which it was intended to deal), and by adopting an interpretation of the words consistent with that purpose; (b) It was generally accepted that the purposive approach applied only when an attempt to apply the literal approach produced an ambiguity or an inconsistency; (c) Under the literal approach, an ambiguity referred to a mistake in the text such as a syntactic or grammatical error, whilst under the purposive approach, an ambiguity extended to circumstances in which the intention of the legislature was, for whatever reason, doubtful.

The court then noted section 15AA of the Acts Interpretation Amendment Act 1980 [Aust] which provides:

In the Interpretation of a provision of an Act, a construction that would promote the purpose or object underlying the Act (whether that purpose or object is expressly stated in the Act or not) shall be preferred to a construction that would not promote that purpose of object.

The following words of Dawson J in the High Court in the case of *Mills v Meeking* [17] pertaining to section 35 of the Victorian Interpretation legislation were quoted with approval:

> The literal rule of construction, whatever the qualifications with which it is expressed, must give way to a statutory injunction to prefer a construction which would promote the purpose of an Act to what which would not . . .The requirement that a court look to the purpose or object of the Act is thus more than an instruction to adopt the traditional mischief or purpose rule in preference to the literal rule of construction... The approach required by section 35 needs no ambiguity or inconsistency; it allows a court to consider the purposes of an Act in determining whether there is more than one possible construction. Reference to the purposes may reveal that the draftsman has inadvertently overlooked something which he would have dealt with had his attention been drawn to it and if it is possible as a matter of construction to repair the defect, then this must be done. However, if the literal meaning of a provision is to be modified by reference to the purposes of the Act, the modification must be precisely identifiable as that which is necessary to effectuate those purposes and it must be consistent with the wording otherwise adopted by the draftsman. Section 35 requires a court to construe an Act, not to rewrite it, in the light of its purposes.[18]

Benjamin J then went on to note Pearce and Geddes's suggestion that Dawson J's comments in *Mills and Meeking* indicated that the provisions relating to the interpretation of legislation had displaced both the literal and purposive common law approaches (the latter being different from the modern purposive approach) and that it was unhelpful to treat those approaches as representing anything more than stages in the development of the principle of interpretation that have current statutory force.[19]

Justice Benjamin finally endorsed the following propositions: (a) Purposive construction is the modern approach to statutory construction: (b) Legislative enactments should be construed so as to give effect to their purpose even if on occasions this may require a strained construction to be placed on legislation; (c) The literal meaning of the legislative text is the beginning, not the end, of the search for the intention of the legislature; (d) Substance should be preferred over form.[20] In applying these principles, the court held without hesitation that the purpose of the provision was to ensure that each party received independent legal advice to ensure that they understood the provisions of the agreement. The court was satisfied that this was the case and that the advice included also the change that had been effected to paragraph 17.

Admittedly, the case of *Black and Black* was dealing with a provision in an interpretation Act which gave guidance as to the approach to be taken. However, it is submitted that this approach has been evolving over time even outside of statute. Driedger's views, which were expressed outside of the context of any statute, as well as the words of Lord Denning in a number of cases indicates that the approach is increasingly preferred. [21] The extent to which the court may go to deal with gaps or omissions is explored in item 3.4.2.11.

3.4 CONTRADICTIONS AMONG RULES OF INTERPRETATION

It is important to remember that for many a classical rule of interpretation that exists, there is another rule whose effect is to counteract the first rule. Lawyers will remember how their professor in a course on introduction to law would have passed around a copy of maxims (or canons) of interpretation in tabular form, one column stating one rule and the other stating a rule that may be cited to neutralize the effect of the other. In practice, the day will be carried not by the side which states the most rules but by the party that convinces a court that his interpretation is more sensible in all the circumstances of the particular case. That is why it is unsafe for a drafter to rely too much, if at all, on rules of interpretation to convey his meaning. Let the rules bail him out where he fails, due to circumstances beyond his control, to fully express himself. It is a common misunderstanding, even among lawyers, that if a rule of interpretation will help clarify an issue, there is no need to put a provision beyond doubt. Perhaps litigation lawyers who make a living arguing cases in a court do not complain if a statute is unclear. However, as far as the drafter is concerned, his call is to make the law as clear as he can without relying on rules of interpretation. For him, he fails if a simple matter that he might have clarified without complications winds up in court.

Generally speaking, the foregoing approaches to interpretation which apply to Acts apply also to statutory instruments. However, by the very nature of statutory instruments, there are certain additional rules that apply which are dictated by the fact that statutory instruments are made under powers conferred by Acts.

3.4.1 INTERPRETATION OF STATUTORY INSTRUMENTS

The main rules governing statutory instruments are nowadays generally contained in an Interpretation Act. One example is the Interpretation Act 1978, [UK]:

11. Construction of subordinate legislation

Where an Act confers power to make subordinate legislation, expressions used in that legislation have, unless the contrary intention appears, the meaning which they bear in the Act.

The wording of this statute excludes cases where "the contrary intention appears". It does not state that the contrary intention must be express. It seems, therefore, that an implied intention is included. For example, if the Fisheries Act defined "fish" as meaning all kinds of sea creatures and the expression is used in the Grouper Regulations, the use of "fish" in those regulations is likely to be and should be construed as referring to grouper unless, again, the context requires otherwise. It may not be so for other reasons – for example, by the application of the golden rule of interpretation summarized at item 3.3.3. Needless to say, where a different definition is used in the statutory instrument, the definition must not be such as to go outside the scope of the Act.

It should follow that if there is a term in the Act which is not defined and a court decision ascribes a meaning to that term, that decision generally holds good where the term is used also in the statutory instrument – unless, again, the context of the particular statutory instrument or provision suggests otherwise.

It is also worth noting that the Interpretation Act, Chapter 1-21, [Can], states:

16. Where an enactment confers power to make regulations, expressions used in regulations have the same respective meanings as in the enactment conferring the power.

In this same Canadian legislation, section 2 (1), the term "regulation" is defined as follows:

"regulation" includes an order, regulation, rule, rule of court, form, tariff of costs or fees, letters patent, commission, warrant, proclamation, by-law, resolution or other instrument issued, made or established (a) in the execution of a power conferred by or under the authority of an Act, or (b) by or under the authority of the Governor in Council.

If only for contrast in the use of terms, the New Zealand provision, section 34 of the Interpretation Act 1999, may also be noted:

A word or expression used in a regulation, Order in Council, Proclamation, notice, rule, bylaw, Warrant, or other instrument made under an enactment has the same meaning as it has in an enactment under which it is made.[22]

The Australians are even more comprehensive:

46 Construction of rules, regulations and by-laws

(1) Where an Act confers upon any authority power to make, grant or issue any instrument (including rules, regulations or by-laws), then:

(a) unless the contrary intention appears, expressions used in any instrument so made, granted or issued shall have the same meanings as in the Act conferring the power, and this Act shall apply to any instrument so made, granted or issued as if it were an Act and as if each such rule, regulation or by-law were a section of an Act; and

(b) any instrument so made, granted or issued shall be read and construed subject to the Act under which it was made, granted or issued, and so as not to exceed the power of that authority, to the intent that where any such instrument would, but for this section, have been construed as being in excess of the power conferred upon that authority, it shall nevertheless be a valid instrument to the extent to which it is not in excess of that power.

(2) Where an Act confers upon an authority power to make an instrument (including rules, regulations or by-laws) or a resolution:

(a) specifying, declaring or prescribing a matter or thing; or

(b) doing anything in relation to a matter or thing;

then, in exercising the power, the authority may identify the matter or thing by referring to a class or classes of matters or things.[23]

It is worth noting that a number of Interpretation Acts provide that the term "Act" includes all statutory instruments made under that Act. Thus when one encounters a provision that says "Any person who commits an offence under this Act for which no penalty is provided shall be liable to a fine of ten thousand dollars", this means that a contravention of a statutory instrument is also covered. This obviates the necessity of always saying (as is usually the intention) "Any person who commits an offence under this Act or any regulations made under this Act . . ."

3.4.2 SOME SPECIFIC RULES

3.4.2.1 IN WHICH CASES DO LAWS BIND THE STATE?

It is a cardinal rule in the interpretation of statutes that a law does not bind the state or, in a monarchical system of government, the Crown, unless the law concerned specifically states so. In some jurisdictions the state or Crown can also be bound by necessary implication. In Canada the rule is expressed as follows:

No enactment is binding on Her Majesty or affects Her Majesty or Her Majesty's rights or prerogatives in any manner, except as mentioned or referred to in the enactment.[24]

The provision in New Zealand is even simpler:

No enactment binds the Crown unless the enactment expressly provides that the Crown is bound by the enactment.[25]

In a republic the provision might be something like the following from the Interpretation Act, Cap. 2, [Zam], section 51 (1):

No written law shall in any manner whatsoever affect the rights of the Republic unless it is therein expressly provided or unless it appears by necessary implication that the Republic is bound thereby.

The Zambian provision seems to make it clear that even if there is no express provision binding the state, this can also be the subject of inference from the subject matter or other evidence of intention that the state should be bound. It is better, however, to have a clear provision requiring express intention that the state be bound. It makes for better clarity in the law and avoids unwitting binding of the state.

Thus when instructions are being given for the drafting of a law, a decision must be made regarding whether the law or particular provisions of it should apply to the state. Policy makers' intentions can be defeated or watered down if the matter is not considered and expressly dealt with as intended.

3.4.2.2 INTERNATIONAL LAW AND NATIONAL LAW

Where a Treaty between two or more countries makes certain provisions in relation to a matter and the provisions of the law of one of the countries are in conflict with the Treaty, the question of which prevails often arises.[26] In the words of Lord Atkin in *Attorney General for Canada v. Attorney General for Ontario,*

Within the British Empire, there is a well established rule that the making of a Treaty is an executive act, while the performance of its obligations, if they entail alteration of the existing law, requires legislative action.

The stipulations of a Treaty do not, by virtue of the Treaty alone, have the force of law. If the government of the day decides to incur the obligations of a Treaty which involves alteration of law they have to run the risk of obtaining the assent of Parliament to the necessary statute or statutes.[27]

This dualist approach, as it is called, sums up the legal position in countries that follow the classical British tradition. The rights and obligations created by a Treaty have no effect in the national or domestic law of a country until the Treaty has been incorporated into that law. When that is done, what applies, in effect, is the law and not the Treaty as such.

The way this operates in practice is as follows.[28] Country A and country B, both island states, enter into an agreement whereby vessels registered in one may enter the fishery waters of the other and catch up to 500 pounds of fish per vessel without a fishing licence from the other state. Person X, whose vessel is registered in country B, is found fishing in the fishery waters of country A without a licence from country A. He has caught fish below the maximum limit.

The fisherman is arrested by marine police officers from country A and charged under its Fisheries Act, wherein it is provided that anyone, without exception as to the pounds of fish caught, who is found fishing without a licence commits an offence. In his defence, X argues that the Treaty has to override the Fisheries Act. The court convicts him nonetheless. The verdict would be right in law, so long as the facts are proved.

Under the European Union, even before the establishment of the European Community and later the European Union, in the 1963 milestone case of *Van Gend en Loos v. Nederlandse Adminstratie der Belastin-*

gen [29] and later cases, the European Court made it clear that the provisions of the treaties of the economic arrangement had direct applicability in the domestic laws of the member countries, conferring rights on individuals, and were, in fact, supreme. In that system, therefore, in the semi-hypothetical case set out above, if the fisheries agreement had been the European Treaty or one of the European Community instruments that have direct applicability in the domestic jurisdictions, the provisions of the agreement would have overridden the provisions of the Fisheries Act.

Since then, however, the United Kingdom has enacted the European Communities Act, 1972, which made statutory provisions further clarifying the position. Section 2 provides that:

(1) All such rights, powers, liabilities, obligations and restrictions from time to time created or arising by or under the Treaties, and all such remedies and procedures from time to time provided for by or under the Treaties, as in accordance with the Treaties are without further enactment to be given legal effect or used in the United Kingdom shall be recognised and available in law, and be enforced, allowed and followed accordingly; and the expression "enforceable Community right" and similar expressions shall be read as referring to one to which this subsection applies.

(2) Subject to Schedule 2 to this Act, at any time after its passing Her Majesty may by Order in Council, and any designated Minister or department may by regulations, make provision –

(a) for the purpose of implementing any Community obligation of the United Kingdom, or enabling any such obligation to be implemented, or of enabling any rights enjoyed or to be enjoyed by the United Kingdom under or by virtue of the Treaties to be exercised; or

(b) for the purpose of dealing with matters arising out of or related to any such obligation or rights or the coming into force, or the operation from time to time, of subsection (1) above;

and in the exercise of any statutory power or duty, including any power to give directions or to legislate by means of orders, rules, regulations or other subordinate instrument, the person entrusted with the power or duty may have regard to the objects of the Communities and to any such obligation or rights as aforesaid.

In this subsection "designated Minister or department" means such Minister of the Crown or government department as may from time to time be designated by Order in Council in relation to any matter or for any purpose, but subject to such restrictions or conditions (if any) as may be specified by the Order in Council.

(3) ...

(4) The provision that may be made under subsection (2) above includes, subject to Schedule 2 to this Act, any such provision (of any such extent) as might be made by Act of Parliament, and any enactment passed or to be passed, other than one contained in this Part of this Act, shall be construed and have effect subject to the foregoing provisions of this section; but, except as may be provided by any Act passed after this Act, Schedule 2 shall have effect in connection with the powers conferred by this and the following sections of this Act to make Orders in Council and regulations.

The Act goes further in section 3 (1) to provide that:

For the purposes of all legal proceedings any question as to the meaning or effect of any of the Treaties, or as to the validity, meaning or effect of any Community instrument, shall be treated as a question of law (and, if not referred to the European Court, be for determination as such in accordance with the principles laid down by and any relevant decision of the European Court).

In the absence of such provisions, no Treaty in a country that follows the classical British practice has direct effect in national law. It must be emphasized, however, that even in the United Kingdom, the treaties and other international obligations entered into outside the European Community (or similar arrangement) generally remain subject to the classical doctrine as it has always been applied in England.

But that doctrine has been coming under strain in different parts of the Commonwealth. Perhaps the most telling in the Caribbean has been the landmark decision of the Caribbean Court of Justice (CCJ) in *Attorney-General and two others v Jeffery Joseph and Lennox Ricardo Boyce*.[30] Some of this strain comes into sharp focus especially when one also reads the separate judgments of Justices Wit and Pollard, who both arrived at the same conclusion as the majority of the court.[31]

There the two applicants were convicted of murder and sentenced to death by hanging under the laws of Barbados. Having lost their appeal before the Barbados Court of Appeal, the Barbados Privy Council (BPC) fulfilled its obligation under section 78 of the Barbados Independence Order 1966, UKSI 1455, by considering the matter. They decided twice not to recommend to the Governor General that the sentence be commuted in exercise of the prerogative of mercy. According to the appellants, the BPC had twice unnecessarily and unduly triggered the issuance of the death warrants. The first time was in June 2002, after the Court of Appeal had dismissed their appeals on 27 March, 2002. The second time was in September 2004, after the Judicial Committee of the Privy Council (JCPC), then the court of final appeal for Barbados, had dismissed their appeals against the mandatory character of their sentences.

At the time of making the second recommendation for a date of execution to be fixed, the attorneys for Joseph and Boyce had filed a complaint with the Inter-American Commission on Human Rights (IACHR). Under that international procedure, the Commission could make a recommendation or ultimately the Inter-American Court of Human Rights could make a decision. The appellants argued that the BPC should in good faith have waited for that procedure to play out before making a decision whether or not to make a recommendation on the granting or denying of mercy. They also argued that the refusal by the BPC to do so amounted to a violation of the fundamental right of "protection of the law" which was said to be equivalent to the entitlement to "due process of law" which was also protected under section 24, the enforcement provision allowing a person to petition if his rights have been, are being or are likely to be violated. Further, they argued that considering four years and four months had already passed after the respondents had been sentenced and that it was highly unlikely that a report of the IACHR would be received within the five-year time frame laid down in the case of *Pratt and Morgan v Attorney-General of Jamaica*, [32] a violation of section 15 of the Jamaican Constitution (prohibiting "inhuman and degrading punishment") was imminent. Finally they submitted that the only relief that could properly be given would be the commutation of the death sentences to life imprisonment.

The American Convention on Human Rights which created the Commission and Court had been signed and ratified by Barbados but it had not been incorporated into the laws of Barbados. One issue was whether ignoring the international procedure amounted to denial of due process in the laws of Barbados. The court considered the dualist doctrine and, while not abrogating it, held that the international procedure was for this purpose part of the law of Barbados in relation to the due process relating to the granting of mercy. In the telling words of Justice Wit: "How could one tell a condemned man, in deadly earnestness, that he exists on two planes and that, although he has a right to stay alive on the one plane, he will be hanged on the other".[33]

This case certainly meted out real justice but its reach must not be overestimated. First, its circumstances were more procedural than substantive. Second, the nature of the case was such that it was possible to imply the international procedure into the laws of Barbados without directly contravening an express provision of any Barbadian law. Third, there was no provision in the Barbados Constitution that specifically contravened the international obligations. Thus whereas students may wish to study the detailed judgments in the case, including the many cases cited there from different parts of the Commonwealth, public officials should be more cautious. It is recommended that unless one operates in a system similar to the EU where direct applicability is firmly established, treaties must be considered as not applying in domestic law unless they have been incorporated by local legislation.[34]

Exotic cases aside, it is trite "that the words of a statute passed after the Treaty has been signed and dealing with the subject-matter of the international obligation . . .are to be construed, if they are reasonably capable of bearing such a meaning, as intended to carry out the obligation and not to be inconsistent with it."[35] Indeed, a court will always try to construe a statute harmoniously with an international obligation regardless of which came first. Needless to say, the presumption may be stronger where the statute was enacted after a country became a party to the Treaty in question.

3.4.2.3 HOW NEW LAWS AFFECT EXISTING RIGHTS

The matter of existing rights is closely related to retrospectivity of legislation. One of the best statements of the meaning of the term and the law affecting it is found in Privy Council case of *Yew Bon Tew v Kenderaan Bas Mera*.[36] There Lord Brighman (delivering the judgment of the Board) had this to say:

> Apart from the provisions of the interpretation statutes, there is at common law a prima facie rule of construction that a statute should not be interpreted retrospectively so as to impair an existing right or obligation unless that result is unavoidable on the language used. A statute is retrospective if it takes away or impairs a vested right acquired under existing laws, or creates a new obligation, or imposes a new duty, or attaches a new disability, in regard to events already past. There is however said to be an exception in the case of a statute which is purely procedural, because no person has a vested right in any particular course of procedure, but only a right to prosecute or defend a suit according to the rules for the conduct of an action for the time being prescribed.
>
> ...
>
> Whether a statute is to be construed in a retrospective sense, and if so to what extent, depends on the intention of the legislature as expressed in the wording of the statute, having regard to the normal canons of construction and to the relevant provisions of any interpretation statute.[37]

Thus there is no general provision in the common law prohibiting retrospective laws. Some Interpretation Acts provide that enactments do not have retrospective effect, meaning that, unless the context otherwise requires, this interpretation must be avoided. Technically, however, it is possible in theory for a Constitution or an international arrangement which establishes a legal order similar to that of the European Union, that is, one which allows international instruments to override national legislation, to prohibit retrospective legislation.

Also, it is important to recognize what kinds of legislation are truly retrospective as to require clear language. A marriage law that changes the legal age for marriage from 18 years to 21 years is not truly retrospective. If this law were to go further and annul marriages (of persons aged 18 to less than 21) that have already taken place, then it would be retrospective and very clear words would be necessary.

3.4.2.4 CONSISTENCY OF LANGUAGE

Where two different expressions are used, there is a presumption that (a) two different meanings were intended and (b) that where a single expression is used repeatedly, the same meaning was intended. In legislation and other legal instruments, elegant variation is an unduly expensive luxury. For instance, if there is reference to "dog" in one part of a law and to "animal" in another, it will be presumed that two different meanings were intended: that "animal" was either not being used to refer to a dog or, depending on context, that it was intended to exclude a dog. In other words, "animal" will be presumed to be broader than "dog". Similarly, if a law refers to "office building" and "building" in different provisions, it will be presumed that "building" was not intended to refer only to an office building.

The presumption, however, is rebuttable – that is, the rule applies unless there is a good reason to suggest why a single meaning may have been intended despite the use of different words. Indeed, no matter how hard a drafter tries to ensure that he abides by the rule, there will be cases where he slips up. This can happen when he uses a particular word early in the legislation and later prefers another one. (Fortunately, this kind of error has become less common now that computer technology enables us to find all the occurrences of a word or phrase and replace it automatically with the preferred one.)

In the above examples, if one wishes to use "dog" and "animal" in different senses, one might say "dog" in one place and in the other "dog or other animal" if that is the intention. Or, if the intention is otherwise, one might say "an animal but not a dog" or words to that effect. If there is no reason for singling out a dog in any particular provision, one may simply use "animal" throughout.

If a drafter does not observe this rule, it does not necessarily follow that his intention will be defeated. What it does mean is that there will be a lot of argument for and against a proposition, with the result that litigation will be bred or some legal advice will have to be given that might have been avoided by making the statute clear. It is the drafter's duty to minimize litigation and even the frequency with which legal advice is sought.

3.4.2.5 GENERAL WORDS AT THE END OF AN ENUMERATION (*EJUSDEM GENERIS* RULE)

There is a general rule of interpretation to the effect that when there are general words at the end of an enumeration and all the items in the preceding list fall into one clear and distinct class, the general words must be restricted to that class. This is a rule of language but also a rule of law. Thus, for example, if a statute stipulates that "no person shall take out of the water grouper, snapper, trout or any other living thing", the words "any other living thing", even if broad enough to cover a whale, will be construed as covering only fish, for the preceding list establishes that class clearly. Naturally, problems may arise when the class is not so distinct. For example, if the provision reads "grouper, snapper, dolphin or other living thing", the class that is established is less clear, since a dolphin is a mammal and the other two elements are not. In that case, it is a question of fact as to whether there is a clear and distinct class in the particular context.

However, the rule is only a general rule. If there are good reasons in the wider context of the Act that make it more sensible to construe it differently, even if the class established is clear and distinct, a court will hold that the particular case is not one to which the rule should apply.

3.4.2.6 ASSOCIATED WORDS (*NOSCITUR A SOCIIS*)

The rule explained above, namely, the *ejusdem generis* rule, applies only where general words are used at the end of an enumeration. There is a sister principle known as *noscitur a sociis* (associated words), which applies in any context. In the words of Stamp J in *Bourne v. Norwich Crematorium*:

> English words derive colour from those which surround them.
> Sentences are not mere collections of words to be taken out of
> the sentence, defined separately by reference to the dictionary or
> decided cases, and then put back again into the sentence with
> the meaning which you have assigned to them as separate words,
> so as to give the sentence or phrase a meaning which as a sen-
> tence or phrase it cannot bear without distortion of the English
> language.[38]

What this means in practice is similar to what was said earlier about the golden rule of interpretation.

The operation of the rule may be illustrated by reference to the Supreme Court of Zambia case of *Rao v. Attorney General*.[39] In that case the court considered the following definition, contained in section 2 of the Preservation of Public Security Act (which has its origins in colonial times):

> "public security" includes the securing of the safety of person
> and property, the maintenance of supplies and services essential
> to the life of the community, the prevention and suppression of

violence, intimidation, disorder and *crime*, the prevention and suppression of mutiny, rebellion and concerted defiance of and disobedience to law and lawful authority, and the maintenance of the administration of justice [Emphasis added].

Under this legislation, one could be detained without trial (with certain safeguards) if he was suspected of committing an act that amounted to a threat to "public security". The problem was to determine whether the large-scale smuggling of emeralds amounted to a threat to public security in a country that was experiencing shortages of foreign exchange. The view of three of the justices was that "crime" covered any kind of crime, including smuggling, while two of the justices where of the view that although "crime" was general enough to cover even petty crime, the meaning of the word had to be narrowed to cover only crimes of the type indicated elsewhere in the definition – that is, crimes that are disruptive of public order at a general level. The articulation of the case for the minority is a good example of the application of the principle of *noscitur a sociis*.

3.4.2.7 TECHNICAL WORDS

There are many terms which exist only in a particular trade, business or profession, and others which mean one thing in everyday usage and have a specialized meaning in a particular trade, business or profession. These are so-called terms of art. In either case, if it is clear that they are being used in a technical sense they must be given the meaning that is ascribed to them in that context. When drafting legislation for a particular class or field of people, terms of art can and, indeed, must be used if that is the best way to convey the intended meaning to the intended audience.

3.4.2.8 ACTS THAT ARE READ NARROWLY

There are certain types of laws that are read narrowly. In legal jargon they are said to be subject to "strict" construction. What are historically called penal statutes are one example. Penal statutes are of two broad kinds: those dealing with criminal law (including arrest and detention), and those dealing with tax. In relation to criminal law statutes, it has been said:

> Where there is an enactment which may entail penal conse-
> quences, you ought not to do violence to the language in order
> to bring people within it, but ought rather to take care that no
> one is brought within it who is not brought within it by express
> language.[40]

Whereas ideally violence should never be done to any language in a statute, regardless of the subject matter, the point should be clear: a court should not easily imply meaning to ensure that an accused is caught by a statute dealing with a criminal matter.

In practice, strict construction means that if there is any doubt about the interpretation of a statute, the doubt must be resolved in favour of the subject. It is for this reason that a statute imposing a tax may read something like "There shall be charged, levied and collected a tax to be known as fuel tax." The words are intended to put it beyond doubt that the money is to be paid and that if it is not paid it can be forcibly exacted. In the words of one judge,

> In a taxing Act one has to look merely at what is clearly said.
> There is no room for any intendment. There is no equity about
> a tax. There is no presumption as to a tax. Nothing is to be read
> in, nothing is to be implied. One can only look fairly at the lan-
> guage used.[41]

Statutes that are read narrowly include those that (a) impose a penalty; (b) authorize arrest and detention; (c) impose a tax, rate or charge; (d) take away vested rights; (e) make a fundamental change in the common law; or (f) take property compulsorily.[42]

The terminology reflects the way taxes were viewed before the advent of the welfare state. Now we accept taxes as necessary to enable the government to provide various amenities. In the days of autocratic monarchical rule, when there was little difference between the monarchy's treasury and that of the state, taxes were seen as unjust enrichment of the monarch. Paying tax was therefore seen as penal – hence the nomenclature.

There is a view that this distinction among statutes need not be maintained. It is said that all that a court should do with all statutes is interpret them in their entire context and give effect to the intention of the law giver. Even if this approach were to become predominant, a court is always likely, due to serious the subject matter of statutes that are said to call for strict construction, to be extra cautious in applying them, whether or not it expressly states that it is applying the principle of strict construction.

3.4.2.9 TAUTOLOGY

Superfluous words are common in statutes. They may owe their presence to habit or to a genuine abundance of caution. A drafter may find it insufficient to refer merely to a "house" and may instead refer to "a house, apartment or other dwelling". Imagine that an issue arises regarding whether a one-room building that is also used as a grocer's shop is a "house or other dwelling". One side may argue that the words "other dwelling" are superfluous and that only a place used exclusively or almost exclusively as a house or apartment is covered. The other may argue that "other dwelling" was added precisely to cover cases such as the one in question. The proper approach is summed up in the words of Viscount Simon in *Hill v. William Hill (Park Lane Ltd)*:

> The rule that a meaning would, if possible, be given to every word in the statute implies that, unless there is good reason to the contrary, the words add something which would not be there if the words were left out.[43]

In the end, therefore, it will again depend on the context in which the words are used in the statute and the purpose of the legislation.

3.4.2.10 USE OF MATERIALS OUTSIDE THE LAW TO UNDERSTAND THE LAW

The use of materials outside the statute itself to help understand it has long been a controversial matter. The principal issues which arise relate mainly to the use of law reform commission reports and parliamentary debates (*Hansard*). Generally speaking, in applying a statute, the courts have historically refused to examine such materials for the purpose of ascertaining the meaning of words in the statute. They were considered unreliable for that purpose. The position at common law, then, has been that the courts could look at such material only to ascertain the mischief that was being investigated.[44]

Latest cases indicate that the general approach relating to extrinsic materials has changed slightly. In *Pepper v. Hart* [45] at least one Law Lord did not preclude the use of a speech made by the person proposing the Bill from being used to find out the meaning of a statute. In another case, *Stubbings v. Webb*,[46] a unanimous decision, the House of Lords considered such a speech as an aid to interpreting some legislation. In that case the Lords, to seek guidance as to the meaning of an Act, did refer to a speech made by a proposer of a Bill and also to the committee recommendations to which the proposer referred. And in the case of *Chief Ad-*

judication Officer v. Foster [47] the House of Lords stated that it was useful to refer to parliamentary material, adding that the cases they referred to indicated "how useful the relaxation of the former exclusionary rule may be in avoiding unnecessary litigation". In all this, the cautionary words of one Law Lord in *Pepper v. Hart* must not be forgotten. He said, "Even in such cases references in court to Parliamentary material should only be permitted where such material clearly discloses the mischief aimed at or the legislative intention lying behind the ambiguous or obscure words." [48] Thus, there is no carte blanche to refer to such material, for in the same case it was also said that

> the exclusionary rule should be relaxed so as to permit reference to Parliamentary material where (a) legislation is ambiguous or obscure, or leads to an absurdity; (b) the material relied upon consists of one or more statements by a minister or other promoter of the Bill together if necessary with such other Parliamentary material as is necessary to understand such statement and their effect; (c) the statements relied upon are clear. [49]

On a broader scale, we should note that some jurisdictions have made statutory provisions in that regard, with the aim of clarifying the position in their jurisdictions. The Acts Interpretation Act 1901 [Aus], section 15AB, stipulates:

> (1) Subject to subsection (3), in the interpretation of a provision of an Act, if any material not forming part of the Act is capable of assisting in the ascertainment of the meaning of the provision, consideration may be given to that material:
>
> > (a) to confirm that the meaning of the provision is the ordinary meaning conveyed by the text of the provision taking into account its context in the Act and the purpose or object underlying the Act;

or

(b) to determine the meaning of the provision when:

(i) the provision is ambiguous or obscure; or

(ii) the ordinary meaning conveyed by the text of the provision taking into account its context in the Act and the purpose or object underlying the Act leads to a result that is manifestly absurd or is unreasonable.

(2) Without limiting the generality of subsection (1), the material that may be considered in accordance with that subsection in the interpretation of a provision of an Act includes:

(a) all matters not forming part of the Act that are set out in the document containing the text of the Act as printed by the Government Printer;

(b) any relevant report of a Royal Commission, Law Reform Commission, committee of inquiry or other similar body that was laid before either House of the Parliament before the time when the provision was enacted;

(c) any relevant report of a committee of the Parliament or of either House of the Parliament before the time when the provision was enacted;

(d) any treaty or other international agreement that is referred to in the Act;

(e) any explanatory memorandum relating to the Bill containing the provision, or any other relevant document, that was laid before, or furnished to the members of, either House of the Parliament by a Minister before the time when the provision was enacted;

(f) the speech made to a House of the Parliament by a Minister on the occasion of the moving by that Minister of a motion that the Bill containing the provision be read a second time in that House;

(g) any document (whether or not a document to which a preceding paragraph applies) that is declared by the Act to be a relevant document for the purposes of this section; and

(h) any relevant material in the Journals of the Senate, in the Votes and Proceedings of the House of Representatives or in any official record of debates in the Parliament or either House of the Parliament.

(3) In determining whether consideration should be given to any material in accordance with subsection (1), or in considering the weight to be given to any such material, regard shall be had, in addition to any other relevant matters, to:

(a) the desirability of persons being able to rely on the ordinary meaning conveyed by the text of the provision taking into account its context in the Act and the purpose or object underlying the Act;

and

(b) the need to avoid prolonging legal or other proceedings without compensating advantage.

For the official, however, this is a minefield, especially in countries where there is no detailed statutory guide on the matter. The law in England and many other countries is still evolving, and the language from the courts has been very guarded. If the official finds it necessary or expedient to refer to any extrinsic material to be sure how the statute should be applied, he must stop and seek legal advice. He can, however, regardless of the jurisdiction in which he is operating, use these Australian provisions or similar provisions as a guide to what he should provide to the legal adviser or drafter when seeking advice or legislation to be drawn.

3.4.2.11 Errors and gaps

Clear drafting errors and other less obvious imperfect expressions of ideas are inevitable in legislation. For example, where clearly a wrong cross-reference is used, the court will always apply it as if the right cross reference was used.[50] Even before the advent of the purposive approach to the statutory interpretation as understood today, courts were able to go further than this to correct obvious mistakes or apply a statute as if certain words had been used or not used.

Maxwell cites a number of early cases relating to errors and gaps.[51] In *The Beta*,[52] an 1869 case, section 374 of the Merchant Shipping Act 1854 provided that no licence granted by Trinity House to pilots "shall continue in force beyond the 31st of January" after its date. It further provided that "the same may . . . be renewed on such 31st day of January in every year, or any subsequent day". Strictly speaking, licences had to be renewed on that date or on a later date. However, the court held that licences could be renewed earlier than 31st January but to take effect from that date. It was said that a strict application would have resulted in a district being left without qualified pilots for days or even weeks.

Even in criminal matters, this has been done. In *Adler v George*[53] it was prohibited to be "in the vicinity of any prohibited place" and obstructing certain persons on duty there. The accused tried to escape conviction by arguing that he was not in the vicinity or neighbourhood of the Royal Airforce station but rather in the actual place. The court applied the provision as if it read "in or in the vicinity".

Outside of such obvious errors or slip-ups, there are many arguable situations as to how far a court can go. In Supreme Court of Canada case of *R v. Shubley* [54] a regulation made under the Correctional Services Act provided that where a criminal investigation is commenced against an inmate, any internal disciplinary proceedings shall be discontinued. Nowhere in the regulation did it also state that the rule should also apply conversely. In a majority decision, the court declined to hold that this was implied. Whereas there were observations that the intention appeared to be aimed at avoiding both disciplinary proceedings and criminal proceedings taking place concurrently, it declined to do so saying that this would amount to inserting words in the statute.

This should illustrate that implying meaning into a statute can be problematic. The cases seem to show that the extent to which a court will go to imply meaning or correct errors depends on a variety of factors including how drastic the change is and the extent of the absurdity or hardship involved. Thus as a practical note for the lay official, it is always best, except in the most obvious of circumstances, to seek a legal opinion from the appropriate agency.

Notes

1. See Article VI of the Constitution of the United States of America; The Commonwealth of Dominica Constitution Order, 1978, UKSI 1027, s 117; the Constitution of Trinidad and Tobago, No 4 of 1976, Ch:01, s 2; s 1 of the Constitution of Barbados as contained in the Barbados Independence Order 1966 UKSI 1455.

2. Driedger, *Construction of Statutes*, (Toronto: Butterworths, 1983), 37.

3. (1971) AC 1 at 10.

4. (1981) 1 All E R 545 at 565.

5. Much of what follows in relation to the four approaches to statutory construction is based on B.H. Simamba,"The Relevance of Economic Crimes to Public Security: A Zambian Case Study" *Lesotho L J* 4, no. 2 (1988): 183–84. Reproduced with permission.

6. (1584) Co Rep 7a; 76 ER 37.

7. Quoted from Sir William Dale, *Legislative Drafting: A New Approach* (London: Butterworths, 1977), 295.

8. See Driedger, *Construction of Statutes*, 75n2.

9. D.R. Miers and A.C. Page, *Legislation* (London: Sweet and Maxwell, 1982), 185.

10. (1884) Cl and Fin 85, 143; 8 ER 1034.

11. (1857) 6 HLC 61, at 106. See also *R. Hydes v Attorney-General* (2000) CILR 206 (Grand Ct, Cayman) where Smellie, C. J. said that statutes *in pari materia* must be construed together as one unified system.

12. (1972) AC 342 at 361.

13. [1993] 1 All ER 42 at 50.

14. 205 FLR 137 [Aust]. At the time of first writing this account, the case was subject to appeal to the Family Court of Australia (Full Court). It was subsequently heard and determined as B v B [2008] FamCAJC 7. That court mentioned but did not disavow the purposive approach. However, it held that there was need for strict compliance. Substantial compliance was not enough as the effect of a valid agreement was to oust the jurisdiction of the court to make adjustive orders. It found that some of the requirements with respect to which a certification was necessary, namely, that the agreement was fair and prudent, had not been complied with. In the circumstances, it found it unnecessary to decide the issue as to whether there was a need to re-execute the certification.

15. Para 125, p 28.

16. *Statutory Interpretation in Australia*, 6th ed, (Chatswood, NSW: LexisNexis, 2006, 22 at [2.5].

17. (1990) 169 CLR 214, at 234-236.

18. Quoted at para 106 of *Black* Case, n14.

19. Quoted at para 107 of *Black* Case, n14.

20. For these propositions see paras 108 and 109, and the cases cited there. Thus cases which have held in the past that words cannot be implied in a statute in the absence of ambiguity or omission are now, generally, of doubtful authority. See for example *de Freitas v Permanent Secretary for the Ministry of Agriculture, Fisheries, Lands and Housing and Others* [1998] 53 WIR 133, Privy Council case coming out of Antiqua and Barbuda. Note also the use of "purposive construction" that is rather different from what it is today: *Fraser v Greenaway* (1992) 41 WIR 136 (East. Carib. Sup. Ct.) where it was said at p 138 that the surrounding circumstances of legislative intent "include the evident object of the statute or section in which the word or phrase under construction appears and the fact that the interpretation of the word or phrase in its primary sense would result in manifest absurdity."

21. See for example Denning in *Magor and St. Mellons Rural District council v. Newport Corp.* [1950] 2 All E R 1226, at 1236 (C.A.) where he said "We sit here to find out the intention of Parliament and of Ministers and carry it out, and we do this better by filling in the gaps and making sense of the enactment than by opening it up to destructive analysis." He was then roundly condemned by the House of Lords but over time this approach has more adherents today.

22. Also Interpretation Act, Cap. 2, [Zam], s 20 (2).

23. Acts Interpretation Act 1901.

24. Interpretation Act, Chapter 1-21, s 17.

25. Section 27, Interpretation Act 1999, [NZ].

26. The sources of international law technically include not just treaties but also customary international law, the general principles of law recognized by civilised nations, and writings of eminent jurists, the

last being a subsidiary source of international law. The other sources will not be discussed here as they are generally of peripheral relevance to the drafting of laws.

27. [1937] AC 326.

28. This illustration is based on an actual case heard by the Eastern Caribbean Court of Appeal, *Acting Chief of Police v. Bryan* (1985) WIR 207. Details have been adjusted to enable us to concentrate only on the facts that are material to an exposition of the principle.

29. (1963) ECR 1. See also B.H. Simamba, *An African Preferential Trade Area: The Institutions, Law and Operations* (Lusaka: University of Zambia Press, 1993), 111, 112.

30. CCJ Appeal No CV 2 of 2005, BB Civil Appeal No 29 of 2004, unreported. There seems to be no system yet for reporting of cases of the CCJ, the cases cited here being available on the Internet marked "Advance Copy".

31. Ibid, unreported. Available separately.

32. (1993) 43 WIR 340; [1994] 2 AC 1.

33. Para 47 of his judgment.

34. See further the judgment of Justice Wit at p 21 et al., and how the courts have tried to avoid the rigid orthodoxy that unincorporated treaties "cannot create rights". These include the presumption that Parliament does not intend to legislate in conflict with its international obligations and even the doctrine of legitimate expectation. In other words, if the government enters into an international obligation, members of the public are entitled to expect that the government will do what it has undertaken internationally.

35. Lord Diplock in *Garland v British Rail Engineering Limited* [1983] 2 AC 751 at 771; also *Regina v Secretary of State for Home Department ex parte Brind and Ors* [1991] AC 696. With respect to Canada see

an endorsement of the same principle in *Pfizer Canada v Canada (Attorney General)* (2003) 224 DLR (4th) 178 (Federal Court of Appeal); *Baker v Canada (Minister of Citizenship and Immigration)* [1999] 2 SCR 817 (Supreme Court of Canada), where the court said that although the Immigration Act did not expressly incorporate language of Canada's obligations under the Convention on the Rights of the Child, in exercising a discretion under the Immigration Act relating to the possible deportation of a mother, the authorities had to take into account the right of the child as one primary consideration in exercising the discretion. It went further to state more generally that values in international human rights law assist in statutory interpretation and judicial review; *Reference Re Public Service Employer Relations Act (Alberta)* [1987] 1 SCR 313, where it was said that in the interpretation of the Canadian Charter of Rights and Freedoms, Canada's international obligations are a "relevant and persuasive factor", para 63, and other cases cited there; and *Canada Ltée (Spraytech Société d'arrosage v Hudson (Town)*[2001] 2 SCR 241 (SCC). In New Zealand see *Tavita v Minister of Immigration* [1994] 2 NZLR 257.

36. [1982] 3 All ER 833. See also the East Caribbean Court case of *Richardson and Others v Richardson* (1995) 50 WIR 178 (from Anguilla); and *A. G. Ebanks v R* (2007) CILR 403, Ct of Appeal, Cayman, where the introduction of a mandatory sentence was held not to amount to a "heavier penalty". Issue of retrospective legislation also considered.

37. At page 836.

38. (1967) 2 All ER 576 at 578.

39. Supreme Court of Zambia Appeal No 24 of 1987; see also discussion of case in Simamba, "Relevance of Economic Crimes to Public Security: A Zambian Case Study". *Lesotho L J* 4, no. 2 (1988):171–97.

40. *Rumbolt v. Schmidt* (1882) 8 QBD 603, Huddleston B at 608.

41. *Cape Brandy Syndicate v. Inland Revenue Commissioners* [1921] 1 KB 64, CA, Rowlatt J at 71.

42. D.J. Gifford and J. Salter, *How to Understand an Act of Parliament* (London: Cavendish, 1996), 129–34.

43. (1949) AC 530, at pp 546, 547; see also Lord Diplock in *Prescold Central Ltd v. Minister of Labour* (1969) 1 WLR 89, at 96, 97.

44. *Murray v. Director of Public Prosecutions* [1994] 1 WLR 1, HL, Lord Mustill at 3. For the origin of the word *Hansard*, see *Stockdale v Hansard* (1839) 9 Ad and E 1; 112 ER 1112; 48 Rev Rep 326.

45. [1993] AC 593, Lord Browne-Wilkinson, at 634 and 640.

46. [1993] AC, HL, at 507.

47. [1993] AC 754, a unanimous decision, see p 772.

48. [1993] AC 593, HL, at 634.

49. Ibid.

50. See materials cited in n51 and cases cited there.

51. Langan, P. St J., *Maxwell on the Interpretation of Statutes*, 3rd ed. (Bombay: NM Tripathi Private Ltd, 1976), 229 et al. See also D. Greenberg, *Craies on Legislation: A Practitioners' Guide to the Nature, Process, Effect and Interpretation of Legislation*, 8th ed. (London: Sweet and Maxwell, 2004), 531-541; and Ruth Sullivan, *Sullivan and Driedger on the Construction of Statutes*, 4th ed. (Toronto: Butterworths, 2002), 29 et al.

52. (1869) 3 Moo. PC (NS) 23. Cited from Maxwell, n51.

53. [1964] 2 QB 7. Also quoted from *Maxwell*, n51.

54. [1990] 1 SCR 3.

CHAPTER 4
FINAL THOUGHT

This publication was not intended to make a master drafter out of any layperson. My aim in this as well as in my earlier book *The Legislative Process: A Handbook for Public Officials* (Bloomington, Indiana: AuthorHouse, 2009) was to make a substantial contribution to the knowledge that a person instructing a drafter needs to have in order to help a drafter's work to the maximum extent possible; the objective being the production of a larger volume of legislation within a given time while not sacrificing quality. Specifically in relation to this book, it is my hope that the official, regardless of the jurisdiction in which he works, will have gained a reasonably good basic insight into the drafting and interpretation of legislation in most jurisdictions of the British Commonwealth.

In trying to delve into issues of drafting and interpretation of legislation as suggested in these pages, the official will find that some drafters do not take kindly to any person who appears to already know that on which they usually advise. Indeed, some will resent this book, seeing it as an attempt to facilitate encroachment into an area that they consider to be their exclusive domain. Above all, therefore, it is important for the instructing official to make his suggestions to the drafter with all the tact that he can muster.

BIBLIOGRAPHY

Books and Articles

Asprey, Michele. *Plain Language for lawyers,* 1999. Sydney, Australia: Federation Press.

_____. Recent Developments in the Plain Language Movement in Australia, a   paper presented to the Fourth Biennial Conference of the PLAIN Language Association International, September 27, 2002, Toronto, Canada.

Bennion, Francis. *Don't Put the Law into Public Hands,* The Times, January 24th 1995.

Coode, George. "On Legislative Expression". Extract from an Appendix to the Report of the Poor Law Commissioners on Local Taxation to Her Majesty's Principal Secretary of State for the Home Department; House of Commons Papers 1843, Vol. 20.

Crabbe, V. R. A. C. *Legislative Drafting.* London: Cavendish, 1993.

Dale, William. *Legislative Drafting: A New Approach.* London: Butterworths, 1977.

Dickerson, F. Reed. *The Fundamentals of Legal Drafting,* 2nd ed. Boston and Toronto: Little, Brown and Company, 1986.

Driedger, Elmer. *The Composition of Legislation – Legislative Forms and Precedents,* 2nd ed. Ottawa, Ontario: Department of Justice,1976.

_____. *Construction of Statutes.* Toronto: Butterworths, 1983.

Gifford, D.J. and Salter, John. *How to Understand an Act of Parliament.* London: Cavendish, 1996.

Gowers, Ernest. *The Complete Plain Words,* 3rd ed. Harmondsworth: Penguin Books, 1987.

Greenberg, D., *Craies on Legislation: A Practitioners' Guide to the Nature, Process, Effect and Interpretation of Legislation,* 8th ed. London: Sweet and Maxwell, 2004.

Langan, P. St J. *Maxwell on the Interpretation of Statutes*, 3rd ed. Bombay: NM Tripathi Private Ltd, 1976.

Miers, D.R., and Page, A.C. *Legislation*. London: Sweet and Maxwell, 1982.

Pearce, D. S., and Geddes. R. S., *Statutory Interpretation in Australia*, 6th ed, Chatswood, N.S.W: LexisNexis, 2006.

Simamba, Bilika H. *An African Preferential Trade Area: The Institutions, Law and Operations*. Lusaka: University of Zambia Press, 1993.

————. "The Experiences of a Drafter in the Legislative Development of Zambia", Namibia Papers, Working Document No. 5, Part I, Centre for African Studies, University of Bremen, 50–63.

————. "The Placing and other Handling of Definitions", *Stat L R* 27, no. 2 (2006): 73 – 82.

————. "The Relevance of Economic Crimes to Public Security: A Zambian Case Study". *Lesotho L J* 4, no. 2 (1988):171–97.

Tiersma, Peter, "The Plain English Movement", http://www.languageandlaw.org/PLAINENGLISH.HTM.

Thornton, G.C. *Legislative Drafting*, 4th ed. London: Butterworths, 1996.

Zander, Michael. *The Law-Making Process*, 6th ed. Cambridge: Cambridge University Press, 2004, 2006. First published 1980.

Other publications

Legislation Manual: Structure and Style, Report 35. Wellington, NZ: Law Reform Commission, May 1996.

Plain English and the Law. Melbourne, Victoria: Law Reform Commission of Victoria, 1987.

Report on the Preparation of Legislation (The Renton Report) (Cmnd. 6053). London, HMSO, 1975).

Further Reading

Books and Articles

Banda, Janet. "Smaller Law Reform Agencies: Prospects and Challenges". *Commonwealth Law Bulletin* 32, no. 4 (December 2006): 595–600.

Barnett, Hilaire. *Constitutional and Administrative Law*, 2nd ed. London: Cavendish, 1999.

Biribonwoha, Pius Perry. "The Role of Legislative Drafting in the Law Reform Process". *Commonwealth Law Bulletin* 32, no. 4 (December 2006): 601–8.

Crabbe, V.R.A.C. *Legislative Drafting*. London: Cavendish, 1993.

———. *Legislative Precedents*. London: Cavendish, 1998.

———. *Understanding Statutes*. London: Cavendish, 1994.

Dick, Robert C. *Legal Drafting in Plain Language*, 3rd ed. Scarborough, Ontario: Carswell, 1995.

Doonan, Elmer. *Drafting*. London: Cavendish, 1995.

Edgar, S.G.G. *Craies on Statute Law*, 7th ed. London: Sweet and Maxwell, 1977.

Greenberg, D. *Craies on Legislation: A Practitioners' Guide to the Nature, Process, Effect and Interpretation of Legislation*, 8th ed. London: Sweet and Maxwell, 2004.

Seidman, R., Seidman, A., and Abeysekere, T. *Legislative Drafting for Democratic Social Change: A Manual for Drafters*. London: Kluwer Law International, 2000.

Seidman, R., Seidman, A., and Payne, J., eds. *Legislative Drafting for Market Reform: Some Lessons from China*. Houndsmills: Macmillan, 1997.

Seidman, R., Seidman, A., and Wälde, T., eds. Making Development Work: Legislative Reform for Institutional Transformation and Good Governance. London: Kluwer Law International, 1999.

Simamba, B.H. "The Experiences of a Drafter in the Legislative Development of Zambia". Namibia Papers, Working Document no. 5, Part I,

Centre for African Studies, University of Bremen, West Germany: 50–63.

———. "The Extending of Investigatory Powers in Zambian Corruption Cases: *Simataa and Another v. Attorney General*". *Lesotho L J* 3, no 2 (1987): 221–33.

———. "Improving Legislative Drafting Capacity". *Commonwealth Law Bulletin* 1125 (2004): 1125–42.

———. "Suspension and Removal of Judges from the East African Court of Justice". *Commonwealth Judicial Journal* 16, no. 1 (June 2005): 4–9.

———. "The Placing and Other Handling of Definitions in Legislation". *Stat L R* 27, no. 2 (2006): 73–82.

———. "The Legality of Legislation by Resolution". *Commonwealth Law Bulletin* 33, no. 1 (March 2007): 15–17.

———. "Should Marginal Notes Be Used in the Interpretation of Legislation?" *Stat L R* 26, no. 2 (2005):125.

———. "To What Extent Can One Deviate from Prescribed Forms without Affecting Their Validity?" *Stat L R* 28, no. 1 (2007): 68.

———. "When Does a Bill Become an Act?" *Commonwealth Law Bulletin* 33, no, 1 (March 2007): 15–17.

Sullivan, R. *Sullivan and Driedger on the Construction of Statutes*, 4th ed. Toronto: Butterworths, 2002.

Williams, Christopher. "The End of the "Masculine Rule"? Gender-Neutral Legislative Drafting in the United Kingdom and Ireland". *Stat L R* 139, no. 3 (2008): 139–153.

Wydick, Richard C. *Plain English for Lawyers*. Durham, NC: Academic Press, 1979.

Other Publications

Amending Forms Manual, 6th ed. Canberra: Office of Parliamentary Counsel, February 2006.

Guide to Legislative Procedures. London: Cabinet Office, October 2004.

Plain English Manual. Canberra: Office of Parliamentary Counsel, 2003.

Statutory Instrument Practice, 4th ed. London: H.M. Stationery Office within the Office of Public Sector Information, November 2006.

Step by Step Guide: Cabinet and Cabinet Committee Processes. Wellington, NZ: Cabinet Office, Department of the Prime Minister and Cabinet, 2001, last updated 2006.

Working with the Office of Parliamentary Counsel: A Guide for Clients, 2nd ed. Canberra: Office of Parliamentary Counsel, July 2002.

Index

Ambiguity, avoidance of

    "above", 2.4.4.4

    "above" and "below", 2.4.2.2

    "abovementioned", 2.4.4.4

    active voice, use of, 2.4.1.3

    "aforesaid", 2.4.4.4

    "aforementioned", 2.4.4.4

    "age", 2.4.4.2

    "and", 2.4.2.5

    "because" clause, 2.4.4.3

    "below", 2.4.4.4

    "commencing" and "ending", 2.4.2.1

    contextual, 2.4.3

    "cross-referencing" in general, 2.4.4.4

    "date", 2.4.4.2

    "despite", 2.4.2.4

    "distance", 2.4.4.2

    "following", 2.4.4.4

    "foregoing", 2.4.4.4

    "from" and "to", 2.4.2.1

    generally, 2.5

    "herein", 2.4.4.4

    "hereinafter", 2.4.4.4

    "hereinbefore", 2.4.4.4

    "heretofore", 2.4.4.4

    "in accordance with", 2.4.2.7

    "last", 2.4.4.4

    "less than" and "more than", 2.4.2.3

    "may", 2.4.2.6

    "modification". *See* "Ambiguous modification"

"next", 2.4.4.4

"not exceeding" and "exceeding", 2.4.2.3

"notwithstanding", 2.4.2.4

"or", 2.4.2.5

"over" and "under", 2.4.2.2

"preceding", 2.4.4.4

rules of interpretation, reliance on, 2.4.4

"said", 2.4.4.4

same words for same thing, 2.4.1.2

"shall" 2.4.2.6

singular, draft in, 2.4.1.1

"subject to", 2.4.2.4

"succeeding", 2.4.4.4

"the provisions of", 2.5.2

"time", 2.4.4.2. *See also* "Computation of time"

"without" clause, 2.4.4.3

Ambiguous modification

adjectives, 2.4.4.1 (a)

adverbs, 2.4.4.1 (b)

clauses, 2.4.4.1 (d)

nationality, involving, 2.4.4.1 (g)

participles, 2.4.4.1 (e)

pronouns, 2.4.4.1 (f)

phrases, 2.4.4.1 (c)

Amendments

Australia, 2.3

citation of Acts that have been amended, 2.3

direct and indirect, 2.3

how to be interpreted, 2.3

in relation to the principal Act, 2.3

marginal notes, 2.3

New Zealand, 2.3

referring to principal Act, 2.3

Atkin, Lord, 3.4.2.2

Australia, Federal

    extrinsic material, use of in interpretation of laws, 3.4.2.10

    English, 2.1

    gender, 2.5.6

    material not forming part of an Act, use of, 3.4.2.10

    subordinate legislation, interpretation of, 3.4.1

Australia, Victoria, 1.4

Browne-Wilkinson, Lord, 3.4.2.10, n29.

Canada

    enactment binding Her Majesty, 3.4.2.1

    gender, 2.5.6

    interpretation of subordinate legislation, 3.4.1

    Law Reform Commission, 1.5

Chapeaux

    opening chapeaux, 2.4.4.4

    terminal chapeaux, 2.4.4.4

Citation of Acts that have been amended, 2.3

Commonwealth (British), English, as official language of, 2.1

Computation of time, 2.4.4.2

Coode, George

    criticism of, 2.2

    the legislative sentence, 2.2

Crime provisions, 2.5.4

Dale, Sir William, 3.3.1, n7

Definitions

    applying only to portion of Act, 2.5.5

    in Acts to apply to subordinate legislation, 2.5.5

    why use definitions, 2.5.5

Dickerson, Reed, 2.4.4.1

Diplock, Lord, 3.4.2.1, n 27

Double negatives, 2.4.5.1

Drafters. *See* "Legislative drafters"

Driedger, E A, 3.2.2; 3.3.1; 3.3.4

Ejusdem generis rule, 2.4.4

Error in legislation, correction of, 2.4.5.2, n 20

European Union, direct application of rules in the UK, 3.4.2.2

Gender, 2.5.6

Gifford, D J, Salter J, 3.4.2.8, n26

Huddleston, B, 3.4.2.8, n24

Indenting, 2.4.4.4

Instructions, rules of statutory interpretation, reliance on, 2.4.4

Intention of Parliament

      as intention of drafter, 3.2.2

      generally, 3.2.1

International agreement. *See* "International law"

International law

      customary international law, 3.4.2.2, n18

      European Union law in the UK, 3.4.2.2.

      when in conflict with national law, 3.4.2.2

Interpretation Act. *See* "Definitions"

Interpretation of statutes

      contradictions among rules of interpretation, 3.4

      ejusdem generis rule, 3.4.2.5

      extrinsic materials, 3.4.2.10

      golden rule, 3.3.1

      international law, 3.7.2.2

      latest approach, 3.3.4

      literal rule, 3.3.1

      mischief rule, 3.3.1

      noscitur a sociis, 3.4.2.6

      presumption as to consistent use of terms, 3.4.2.3

      strict construction, 3.4.2.8

subordinate legislation, 3.4.1

tautology, 3.4.2.9

technical words, 3.4.2.7

Latin maxims and expressions

discouragement of, 2.5

Ejusdem generis, 2.4.4

mutatis mutandis, 2.5

Legislative Counsel. *See* "Legislative drafters"

Legislative drafters

as players in "the intention of Parliament", 3.2.2

Legislative language

complexity of, 1.2

criticism of, 1.1

England, used in, 1.2

plain language. *See* "Plain English movement"

Legislative proposals. *See* "Instructions"

Mustill, Lord, 3.4.2.10, n28

New Zealand

amendments, 2.3

enactment binding the Crown, 3.4.2.1

English, 2.1

gender, 2.5.6

interpretation of subordinate legislation, 3.4.1

subordinate legislation, meaning of words use in, 3.4.1

Parliament

intention of, 3.2.1

subordinate legislation, in relation to, 3.2.1

supremacy of, 3.2.1

Parliamentary Counsel. *See* "Legislative drafters"

Plain English movement

United Kingdom, 1.5

United States, 1.5

general, 1.4

Victoria, Australia, 1.4

Powers

how to confer, 2.4.1.3

Punctuation

apostrophe, 2.4.5.3 (e)

colon, 2.4.5.3 (c)

colon and dash, 2.4.5.3 (c)

comma in general, 2.4.5.3 (b)

full-stop, 2.4.5.3 (a)

hyphen, 2.4.5.3 (f)

parenthesis, 2.4.5.3 (b)

semi-colon, 2.4.5.3 (d)

Renton Committee, 1.3

Rules of drafting. *See* "Ambiguity, avoidance of"

Simamba, B H, 2.5.5 n23; 3.3, n5; 3.4.2, n21; 3.4.2.6, n23

Simon, Lord, 3.3.4

Simon, Viscount, 3.4.2.9

Stamp, J, 3.4.2.6

Statutory bodies, 2.5.3

Structural check, 2.6

Thornton, G C, 2.2; 2.4.2.4; 2.4.2.5; 2.4.4.1 (b); 2.4.4.4

United Kingdom,

English, 2.1

interpretation of subordinate legislation, 3.4.1

subordinate legislation, interpretation of, 3.4.1

Vagueness

deliberate use of, 2.4.4

Voice

active, in general, 2.5.1

active voice to confer a power, 2.4.1.3

passive, 2.5.1

Wensleydale, Lord, 3.2.2

Wilberforce, Lord, 3.2.2

Zambia

  interpretation of amendments, 2.3

  written law binding the Republic, 3.4.2.1

www.ingramcontent.com/pod-product-compliance
Lightning Source LLC
Chambersburg PA
CBHW022231290526
45785CB00014B/508